Teaching Pal 4

Authors and Advisors

Alma Flor Ada • Kylene Beers • F. Isabel Campoy
Joyce Armstrong Carroll • Nathan Clemens
Anne Cunningham • Martha Hougen
Elena Izquierdo • Carol Jago • Erik Palmer
Robert Probst • Shane Templeton • Julie Washington

Contributing Consultants

David Dockterman • Mindset Works
Jill Eggleton

Navigating the Teaching Pal

The Teaching Pal is a companion to the Teacher's Guide, providing point-of-use instructional notes for using the student texts in *my*Book for different purposes.

Blue Notes
READ FOR UNDERSTANDING

During a first reading of the complete text, use these notes to guide collaborative discussion about the gist of the text.

 READ FOR UNDERSTANDING

ASK: Why is Dilly alone? *(Possible responses: Minna could not swim as fast as Dilly; Dilly was having so much fun, he didn't think about where he was going.)*

ANNOTATION TIP: Have children underline the words that tell how Dilly feels.

FOLLOW-UP: What do you think Dilly will do? *(Accept reasonable responses.)*

DOK 2

Purple Notes
TARGETED CLOSE READ

During subsequent readings, use these notes to take a closer look at sections of the text to apply a reading skill.

 TARGETED CLOSE READ

Characters

Have children reread pages 70–71 to identify the story characters.

ASK: Who are the characters in the story? *(two friends, Dilly and Minna)*

FOLLOW-UP: What do you know about them? *(Dilly looks different from Minna and the other ducks; Dilly and Minna like to have fun together.)*

ANNOTATION TIP: Have children underline the words that describe Dilly.

DOK 3

Yellow Notes

Use these notes for teaching support on the pages that appear before and after each text.

Academic Discussion

Use the TURN AND TALK routine. Remind children to follow agreed-upon rules for discussion, such as taking turns speaking and adding to their partner's ideas.

Possible responses:

- Why was Dilly bigger than the other ducks? Would Dilly ever see Minna again? **DOK 1**
- Even though Dilly looks different, he is still special. **DOK 2**

Red Notes
NOTICE & NOTE

Use these notes to help children learn to look for signposts in a text in order to create meaning.

Notice & Note

Contrasts and Contradictions

Remind children that when a character acts or feels differently than we expect, the author is showing us something important about the character.

Tell them that when that happens, they should stop to notice and note, which includes asking themselves questions about what they read.

Have children explain why they might use this strategy on pages 72–73. *(Dilly was always happy, but now he is sad and afraid.)*

Remind them of the Anchor Question: **Why might Dilly feel this way?** *(He is alone and lost.)*

DOK 2

TABLE OF CONTENTS

MODULE 7

The Big Outdoors

🌱 **SCIENCE CONNECTION:** The Natural World 8

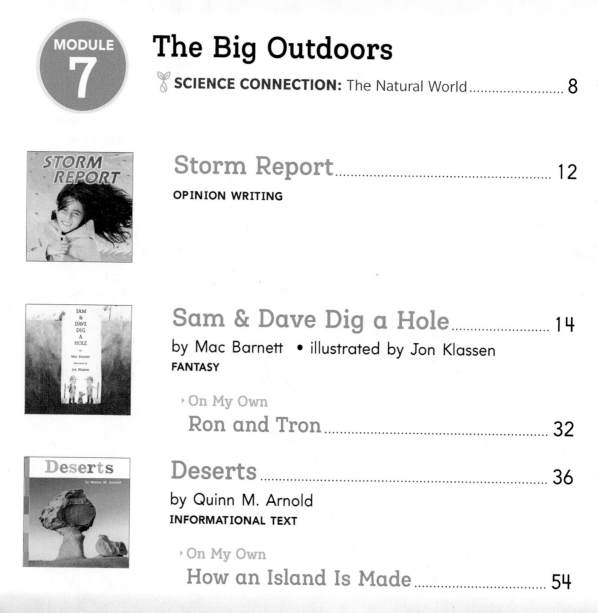

Storm Report 12
OPINION WRITING

Sam & Dave Dig a Hole 14
by Mac Barnett • illustrated by Jon Klassen
FANTASY

› On My Own
Ron and Tron 32

Deserts 36
by Quinn M. Arnold
INFORMATIONAL TEXT

› On My Own
How an Island Is Made 54

4

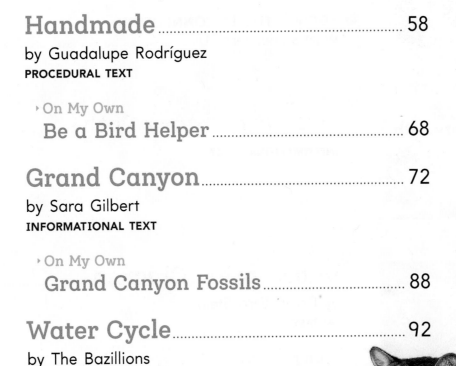

Handmade 58
by Guadalupe Rodríguez
PROCEDURAL TEXT

› On My Own
Be a Bird Helper 68

Grand Canyon 72
by Sara Gilbert
INFORMATIONAL TEXT

› On My Own
Grand Canyon Fossils 88

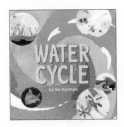

Water Cycle 92
by The Bazillions
MEDIA: SONG

Let's Wrap Up! 96

MODULE

8

Tell Me a Story

🌐 **SOCIAL STUDIES CONNECTION:**
What Stories Teach Us 98

Follow the Story Path 102
INFORMATIONAL TEXT

Interrupting Chicken 104
by David Ezra Stein
FANTASY

› On My Own
Hansel and Gretel Two 134

Little Red Riding Hood 138
by Lisa Campbell Ernst • illustrated by Jesús Aguado
DRAMA

› On My Own
Keep Trying 158

6

The Grasshopper & the Ants 162
by Jerry Pinkney
FABLE

> ▸ On My Own
A Tale of Two Mice 188

Thank You, Mr. Aesop 192
by Helen Lester • illustrated by Roberto Weigand
INFORMATIONAL TEXT

> ▸ On My Own
Make Stories Come Alive 202

The Tortoise and the Hare 206
from Speakaboos, adapted by Amy Kraft
MEDIA: VIDEO

Let's Wrap Up! 210

Glossary 212

Index of Titles and Authors 223

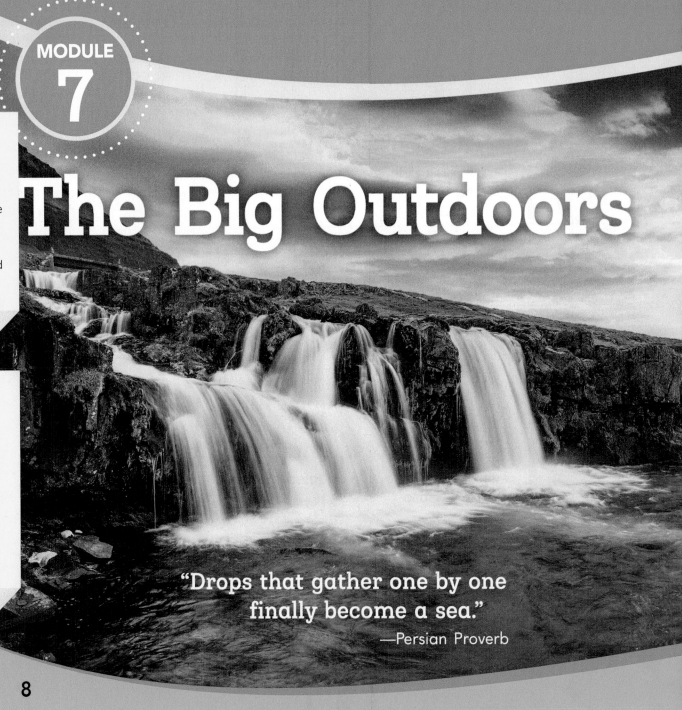

MODULE

7

The Big Outdoors

Introduce the Topic

- **Read aloud** the module title, *The Big Outdoors*.

- **Tell children** that in this module they will be reading texts about the natural world.

- **Have children** share prior knowledge about the topic or word associations for the natural world. Record their ideas in a web.

Discuss the Quotation

- **Read aloud** the Persian proverb.

- **Lead a discussion** in which children try to explain the quote in their own words. Explain the meaning as needed: *A big change can happen when many smaller things come together.*

ASK: What little things in nature can change into something big?
(Accept reasonable responses.)

"Drops that gather one by one finally become a sea."
—Persian Proverb

8

Essential Question

How do things in nature change?

Introduce the Essential Question

- **Read aloud** the Essential Question.
- **Explain that in this module** children will gather and think about information from what they read to help them answer the question.

View and Respond to a Video

Use the ACTIVE VIEWING routine with the Get Curious Video: *Water in the Desert*.

Get Curious Video

9

Words About the Natural World

Complete the Vocabulary Network to show what you
know about the words.

cycle

Meaning: A **cycle** is a group of events that repeat
in the same order.

Synonyms and Antonyms	Drawing

evaporation

Meaning: **Evaporation** is when something gets very hot and turns into a gas.

Synonyms and Antonyms	Drawing

liquid

Meaning: A **liquid** is something that you can pour, like water or milk.

Synonyms and Antonyms	Drawing

Vocabulary Network

- **Point out** to children that they could draw a diagram of what happens to a puddle on a hot day to illustrate *evaporation*.

- **As children complete** the activity for *liquid*, encourage them to think about things that people can drink and things that can be poured.

11

STORM REPORT

READ together

📖 READ FOR UNDERSTANDING

Introduce the Text

• **Read aloud** the title, *Storm Report*. Tell children that it is opinion writing. Ask them to recall what they know about opinion writing. *(It tells an author's thoughts, beliefs, or ideas.)*

• Guide children to **set a purpose**.

• **Read the text** with children.

DOK 3

📖 READ FOR UNDERSTANDING

Ideas and Support

ASK: What does the author want readers to do? *(Read the book* Big Storms.*)*

FOLLOW-UP: What can you learn about by reading the book? *(You can learn about different kinds of storms.)*

ANNOTATION TIP: Have children underline the names of the storms you can learn about in the book. Then have them draw a line from the name of the storm to the photo of that storm on p. 13.

DOK 3

The clouds get dark.
The wind blows.
FLASH! BOOM!
It's a storm!

Do you want to find out about storms? Then read a great book called Big Storms. It is about all kinds of powerful storms. Big snowstorms are called blizzards. There are even big dust storms!

You will see exciting photos of real storms. One picture shows a huge bolt of lightning. Another one shows a blizzard. The snow is up to the windows of the houses!

12

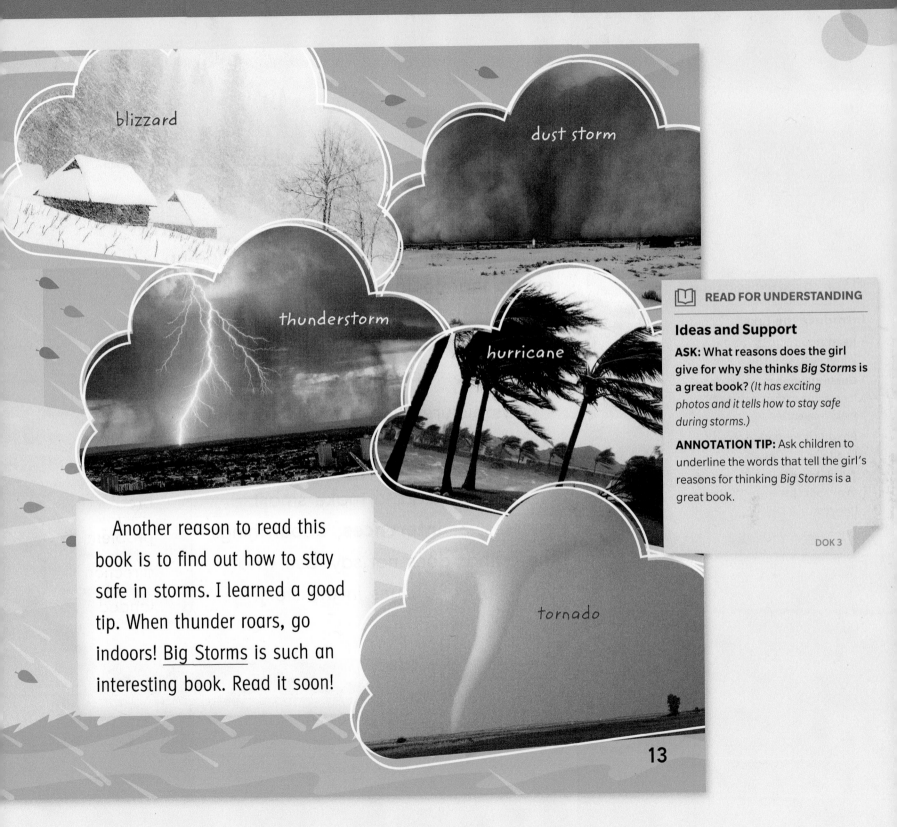

blizzard

dust storm

thunderstorm

hurricane

Another reason to read this book is to find out how to stay safe in storms. I learned a good tip. When thunder roars, go indoors! <u>Big Storms</u> is such an interesting book. Read it soon!

tornado

13

READ FOR UNDERSTANDING

Introduce the Text

• **Read aloud** and discuss the information about the genre.
• **Guide children** to set a purpose for reading to practice how to make inferences.
• **Provide information** about the illustrator, Jon Klassen.
• **Tell children** to look for and think about the Power Words as they read.

Prepare to Read

GENRE STUDY **Fantasy** stories have made-up events that could not really happen. Look for:

• make-believe parts of the setting and events
• problems and resolutions
• ways pictures and words help you understand the story

SET A PURPOSE Read to make smart guesses, or **inferences**, about things the author does not say. Use what you know and clues in the story.

POWER WORDS

mission

spectacular

break

problem

direction

landed

Meet Jon Klassen.

14

SAM
&
DAVE
DIG
A
HOLE

by

Mac Barnett

illustrated by

Jon Klassen

📖 **READ FOR UNDERSTANDING**

Make Predictions

- **Page through** the beginning of *Sam & Dave Dig a Hole* with children.
- Have them **use prior knowledge**, what they know about the characteristics and structure of fantasies, and the illustrations to predict what the story will be about. Tell children they will **return to their predictions** after they finish reading the story.

DOK 2

📖 **READ FOR UNDERSTANDING**

Concept Words

As children read *Sam & Dave Dig a Hole,* they may see familiar words from their speaking and listening vocabularies that they may not know how to read yet. Write these words on the board, read them aloud, and discuss their meanings as needed.

- deep
- digging
- dirt
- tired
- underground

On Monday Sam and Dave dug a hole.

📖 READ FOR UNDERSTANDING

ASK: Who are Sam and Dave? *(two boys who are friends and do things together)*

FOLLOW-UP: What evidence tells you this? *(The picture shows two boys holding shovels. The text says that Sam and Dave dug a hole.)*

DOK 2

16

"When should we stop digging?" asked Sam.
"We are on a mission," said Dave.
"We won't stop digging until we find
something spectacular."

READ FOR UNDERSTANDING

ASK: Where do Sam and Dave start
their mission? *(in their yard, near an
apple tree)*

DOK 1

17

Make Inferences

MODEL MAKING AN INFERENCE

💬 **THINK ALOUD** *The text says that Dave and Sam still haven't found anything spectacular. In the picture, a spectacular diamond is buried close by. I can use these clues to make an inference. I think that the author is letting readers know something that Sam and Dave don't know so that they will stay interested and keep reading!*

DOK 2

🔍 **TARGETED CLOSE READ**

Point of View

Have children reread pages 18–19 to identify the story's point of view.

ASK: Is the narrator a character in the story? *(No, it is someone who is not in the story.)*

FOLLOW-UP: How do you know? *(The narrator tells about both characters and uses the words their and they.)*

ANNOTATION TIP: Have children circle the words that help them understand who the narrator is.

DOK 3

The hole got so deep that their heads were underground.
But they still had not found anything spectacular.
"We need to keep digging," said Dave.

18

So they kept digging.

READ FOR UNDERSTANDING

Make Inferences

ASK: What does the dog know that Sam and Dave don't know? *(that Sam and Dave missed something spectacular)*

FOLLOW-UP: What evidence lets you know? *(The picture shows the dog looking toward a big diamond near where the boys are digging.)*

ANNOTATION TIP: Have children draw a line from the dog's eyes to the spectacular diamond it is looking at.

DOK 2

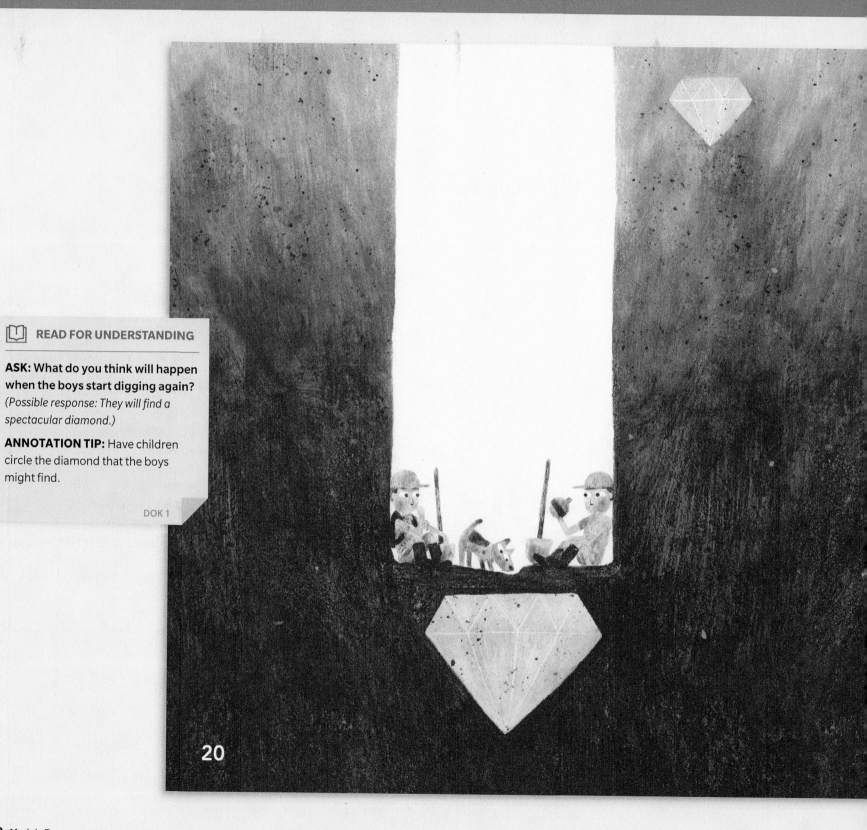

20

They took a break.
Dave drank chocolate milk
out of a canteen.
Sam ate animal cookies he had wrapped
in their grandfather's kerchief.
"Maybe," said Dave,
"the problem is that we are
digging straight down."
"Yes," said Sam.
"That could be the problem."
"I think we should dig in
another direction," said Dave.
"Yes," said Sam.
"That is a good idea."

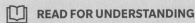

READ FOR UNDERSTANDING

ASK: Do you think Sam and Dave's idea will work? Why or why not? (Accept reasonable responses.)

FOLLOW-UP: What do you think they should do? (Possible response: They should keep digging straight down so that they can find the diamond that is below them.)

DOK 1

21

"I have a new idea," said Dave.
"Let's split up."
"Really?" said Sam.
"Just for a little while," said Dave.
"It will help our chances."

So Dave went one way,

and Sam went another.

READ FOR UNDERSTANDING

ASK: What does the phrase *split up* mean? *(to go in different directions)*

FOLLOW-UP: What clues help you figure out the meaning? *(The text says that Dave went one way and Sam went another; the picture shows them digging in different directions.)*

DOK 2

22

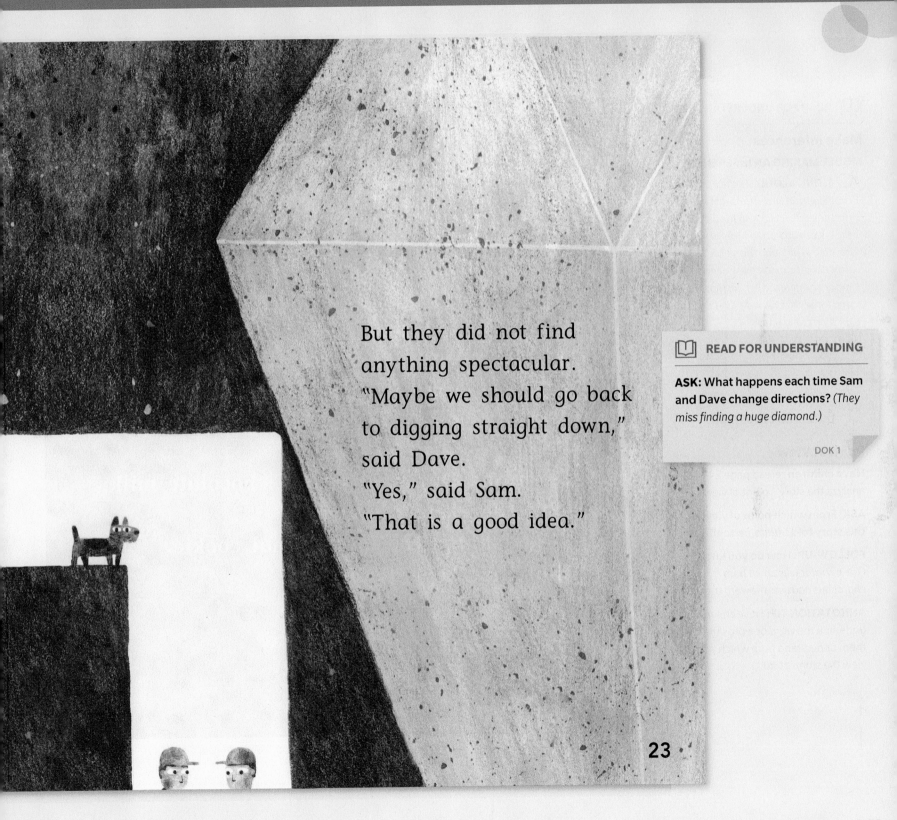

But they did not find anything spectacular.
"Maybe we should go back to digging straight down," said Dave.
"Yes," said Sam.
"That is a good idea."

📖 READ FOR UNDERSTANDING

ASK: What happens each time Sam and Dave change directions? *(They miss finding a huge diamond.)*

DOK 1

23

Make Inferences

MODEL MAKING AN INFERENCE

💬 **THINK ALOUD** *The text says that Sam and Dave ran out of milk and animal crackers. In the picture, the boys' clothes and faces are covered in dirt, and the hole is now very deep. I can use these clues to make an inference. I think that Sam and Dave have been digging the hole for a very long time!*

DOK 2

🔍 **TARGETED CLOSE READ**

Point of View

Have children reread page 24 to analyze the story's point of view.

ASK: From which point of view is this story told? *(third-person)*

FOLLOW-UP: How do you know? *(The narrator tells about both characters and uses the word* they.*)*

ANNOTATION TIP: Have children underline the word or words that help them understand from which point of view the story is told.

DOK 3

Sam and Dave ran out of chocolate milk.
But they kept digging.
They shared the last animal cookie.
But they kept digging.

24

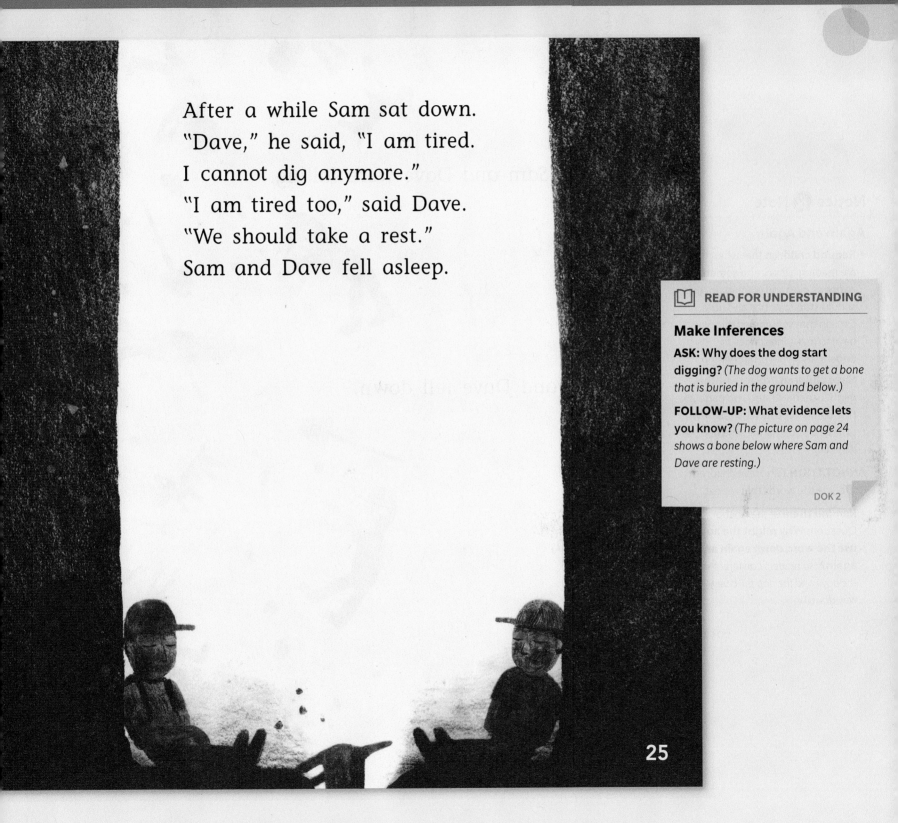

After a while Sam sat down.
"Dave," he said, "I am tired.
I cannot dig anymore."
"I am tired too," said Dave.
"We should take a rest."
Sam and Dave fell asleep.

25

Again and Again

- **Remind children** that when they are reading a story and something happens over and over again, they should stop to notice and note. Explain that sometimes they will have to make inferences to understand what is happening.

- **Have children** explain why they might use the strategy on page 26. *(The author repeats the word* down *to describe how far the boys and the dog fall.)*

ANNOTATION TIP: Have children underline the words that repeat.

- **Remind them** of the Anchor Question: **Why might the author use the word** *down* **again and again?** *(so readers can infer that the boys and the dog fall a very long way down)*

DOK 2

Then Sam and Dave were falling.

Sam and Dave fell down,

down,

down,

26

until they landed in the soft dirt.

"Well," said Sam.
"Well," said Dave.
"That was pretty spectacular."

27

Make Inferences

ASK: Where do Sam and Dave land? *(in a place that looks almost just like their home)*

FOLLOW-UP: How do you know they are not back home? *(They started digging near an apple tree, but they end up near a pear tree. The flower on the porch is different, the weathervane is different, and the cat has a different-colored collar.)*

ANNOTATION TIP: Have children circle the details in the illustration that show that Sam and Dave are not back at home.

DOK 2

Make Inferences

ASK: Do Sam and Dave know they are not back at home? *(no)* Does the dog know? *(yes)*

FOLLOW-UP: How do you know? *(The text says that Sam and Dave go inside for more milk and animal crackers and the picture shows them walking toward the house; the dog is looking at the pear tree with a knowing look on its face.)*

DOK 2

Wrap Up

Revisit the predictions children made before reading. Have them confirm or correct their predictions using evidence from the text and pictures.

DOK 2

And they went inside
for chocolate milk and animal cookies.

Turn and Talk

READ
Together

Use details from **Sam & Dave Dig a Hole** to answer these questions with a partner.

1. **Make Inferences** How can you tell that the boys are good friends?

2. What makes the boys' adventure spectacular?

Talking Tip

Take turns talking. When it is your turn, add on to your partner's idea.

My idea is _____.

29

READ Together

Write a Message

PROMPT Think of a part of the story when Sam and Dave almost find something spectacular. What message could you send to them to help them find it?

PLAN Draw a map. Show where Sam and Dave are and how to get to the spectacular thing.

Write About Reading

• **Read aloud** the prompt.

• **Lead a discussion** in which children share their ideas about messages they could send to Sam and Dave. Tell them to use text evidence to support their ideas.

• Then read aloud the Plan section. Have children use ideas from the discussion in their maps.

DOK 2

WRITE Now write a message to Sam and Dave. Tell them how to find the spectacular thing. Remember to:

- Use a capital letter to begin each sentence and to write the word **I**.

- Use words to tell which way to go, like **left, right, up, down, above,** and **below**.

Responses may vary.

Write About Reading

- **Read aloud** the Write section.
- **Encourage children** to use their maps to help them as they choose which direction words to use in their messages. Also encourage them to capitalize the first word in a sentence and the pronoun *I*.

DOK 2

31

Independent Close Reading

Have children close read and annotate "Ron and Tron" on their own during small-group or independent work time. As needed, **use the Scaffolded Support notes** that follow to guide children who need additional help.

Scaffolded Support

As needed, remind children to:

- look for clues in the text and pictures to help them make inferences to understand things the author does not say.

- look for clues that will help them identify from whose point of view the story is told and whether or not its narrator is a character in the story.

DOK 3

Prepare to Read

GENRE STUDY **Fantasy** stories have made-up events that could not really happen.

MAKE A PREDICTION Preview **Ron and Tron**. Ron and Tron live on different planets. Think about how fantasy stories have make-believe events. What do you think will happen?

The two robots will find treasure.

SET A PURPOSE Read to find out what Ron and Tron do and to see if your prediction is right. If not, think about what a fantasy story is like and make a new prediction.

Ron and Tron

READ Does a narrator outside the story or a character in the story tell the very beginning? How do you know? Who writes the letter? Circle words that help you know who is telling this part of the story.

Ron and Tron live far away from each other. They write to keep in touch.

Hi Tron,
    Last week, I was digging deep under the sea on my planet. I found red and green gems! They glow and sparkle. You like to dig for gems too, so come visit me!
          Your friend,
          Ron ▶

Close Reading Tip

Is your prediction right so far? If not, think about the genre and make a new prediction.

Scaffolded Support

As needed, remind children that:

- stories can be told from the first- or third-person point of view, and that the narrator and/or point of view can change.

- they should reread the text to look for important ideas.

DOK 2

33

READ Who tells the part of the story at the top of the page? Circle words that help you know. Does a character in the story or a narrator outside the story tell the end? How do you know?

Close Reading Tip

Did your prediction match what happened in this story? What were you right about? What was different?

Hi Ron!

You are right! I DO like to dig and explore. But do you want to come visit me first? We can help each other look for gems in the deep, dark caves on my planet.

Your pal,

Tron

Ron went to Tron's planet. They looked in the caves. No gems! But they found lots of bats and had a good time anyway.

CHECK MY UNDERSTANDING

Ron and Tron found bats because

the planet has caves

and bats live in them.

WRITE ABOUT IT How can you tell that Ron and Tron are friends? Write sentences. Use details from the story to explain why.

Ron and Tron call each other friend and pal. They like to do things together, like dig and explore. They both like gems.

35

READ Together

Introduce the Text

- **Read aloud** and discuss the information about the genre.
- **Guide children** to set a purpose for reading to practice monitoring and clarifying as they read.
- **Provide information** about the background topic, Water Matters!
- **Tell children** to look for and think about the Power Words as they read.

Prepare to Read

GENRE STUDY **Informational text** is nonfiction. It gives facts about a topic. Look for:

- facts about the world
- photos with labels
- ways pictures and words help you understand the text

SET A PURPOSE As you read, stop and think if you don't understand something. Reread, look at the pictures, use what you already know, or ask yourself questions.

POWER WORDS

dunes

shrubs

spines

rest

Build Background: Water Matters!

36

Deserts

by Quinn M. Arnold

Hello, desert!

Hot deserts are dry. They do not get much rain.

38

The biggest hot desert is the Sahara.

📖 READ FOR UNDERSTANDING

ASK: What can the desert be like?
(rocky or sandy)

FOLLOW-UP: How do you know?
(The words say that deserts may be rocky or sandy; the photo shows a desert that has sand and rocks.)

ANNOTATION TIP: Have children underline the words that describe what a desert can be like.

DOK 2

🔍 TARGETED CLOSE READ

Central Idea

Have children reread pages 40–41 to analyze the central idea of the text.

ASK: What is this text about?
(deserts)

FOLLOW-UP: What evidence helps you understand this? *(The text describes what deserts look like; the photo shows a desert.)*

DOK 2

Deserts may be rocky or sandy. Sometimes they have rocks and sand.

Sandy deserts may
have tall dunes.
Snakes slide over
the sand.

41

Plants and animals adapt to the desert. Animals get water from food they eat.

📖 **READ FOR UNDERSTANDING**

Quick Teach Words

As needed to support comprehension, briefly explain the meaning of *adapt* in this context.

• If plants and animals *adapt* to a place, they change their behavior so that it is easier for them to live in that place.

📖 **READ FOR UNDERSTANDING**

Phonics/Decoding in Context

Have children point to the word *eat*. Review that the vowel team *ea* can stand for the long vowel sound /ē/. **Model blending** the sounds in the word: /ē/ /t/, *eat*. Have children repeat.

ANNOTATION TIP: Have children circle *ea* in *eat*. Then have them find and circle another word with the vowel team *ea* on page 43. *(reach)*

Shrubs and wildflowers have long roots. They can reach water far below.

📖 **READ FOR UNDERSTANDING**

Monitor and Clarify

MODEL MONITORING AND CLARIFYING

🗨 **THINK ALOUD** *I'm not sure why these shrubs and wildflowers need to get water from deep below the desert. What can I do to make sure I understand? I can ask myself a question, think about what I already know, reread, and look at the photo. I'll try going back and rereading a few pages. Now I understand! Deserts don't get much rain. They are rocky and sandy. So the plants need to reach down deep to find water.*

DOK 2

43

Numbers and Stats

- **Remind children** that when an author uses specific numbers, they should stop to notice and note. Tell them they can use fix-up strategies, such as rereading, asking questions, and looking at the photos to help them understand why this information is important.

- **Have children** explain why they might use this strategy on page 44. *(The author uses the phrase "more than 40 feet tall" to describe how big some cacti can grow.)*

ANNOTATION TIP: Have children underline the number and words used to describe the size of the cacti.

- **Remind them** of the Anchor Question: **What does this make me wonder about?** *(Possible response: I wonder what other things are 40 feet tall. I wonder how cacti store the water.)*

DOK 2

Some cacti grow more than 40 feet tall. They store water.

44

Sharp spines
keep many
animals away.

45

The hot desert sun warms lizards.

46

Jackrabbits rest in shade.
Foxes come out of their
dens at night.

📖 **READ FOR UNDERSTANDING**

ASK: Why do you think these animals stay in the shade or come out at night? (*Possible response: It's too hot for them during the day.*)

FOLLOW-UP: How are they different from lizards? (*They have fur that keeps them warm.*)

ANNOTATION TIP: Have children underline the names of the desert animals on pages 46 and 47.

DOK 2

Picture a Desert

Sahara Desert

dune

palm tree

scorpion

sand

📖 **READ FOR UNDERSTANDING**

ASK: What do the photos on pages 48–49 show? *(the Sahara and the Sonoran deserts)*

FOLLOW-UP: What do the labels help you understand? *(what each desert is like, and what plants and animals live in each one)*

ANNOTATION TIP: Have children underline the labels that name animals and circle the labels that name plants.

DOK 2

🔍 **TARGETED CLOSE READ**

Central Idea

Have children reread pages 48–49 to analyze the central idea of the text.

ASK: What does the author want you to learn from this text? *(that many different plants and animals live in deserts)*

FOLLOW-UP: How do the photos and labels help you figure out the central idea? *(They show what the desert, animals, and plants look like.)*

DOK 2

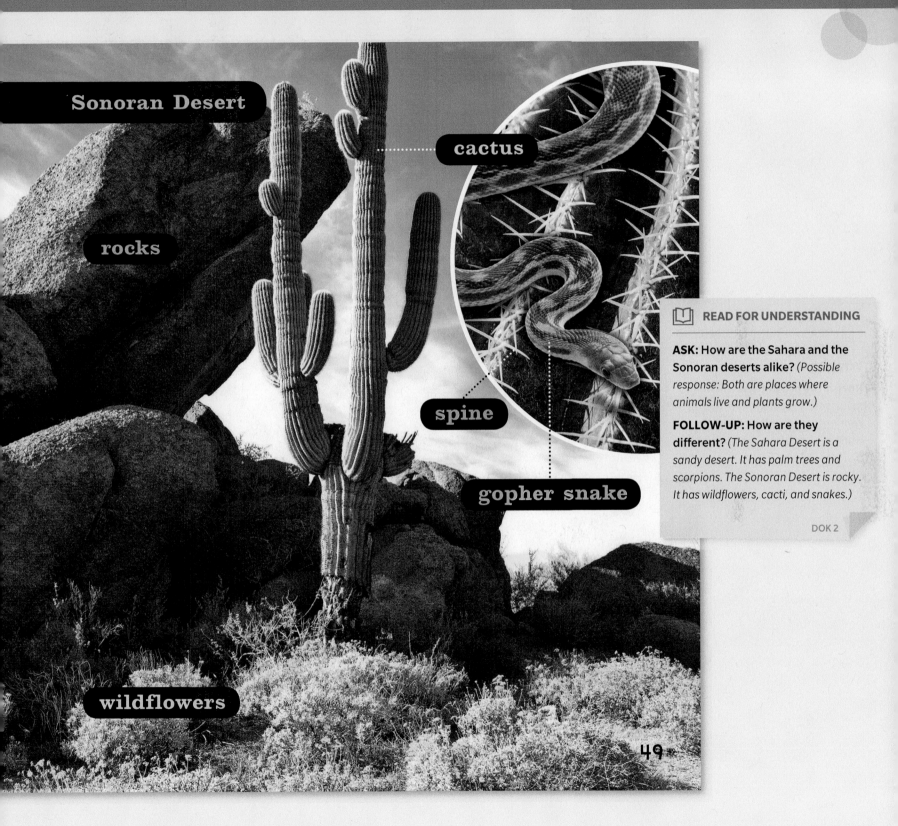

Sonoran Desert

cactus

rocks

spine

gopher snake

wildflowers

49

Wrap Up

Revisit the predictions children made before reading. Have them confirm or correct their predictions using evidence from the text and pictures.

DOK 2

Goodbye, desert!

50

READ Together

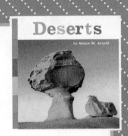

Deserts

Turn and Talk

Use details from **Deserts** to answer these questions with a partner.

1. **Monitor and Clarify** When you came to a part you did not understand, what did you do to figure it out?

2. How do animals get food, water, and shelter in a desert?

Listening Tip

Listen carefully. Think about what your partner is saying and what you learn.

51

Write a Description

PROMPT How can you describe the land or a living thing from **Deserts** for someone who has never seen it? Use details from the words and photos to explain.

PLAN First, write your topic. Then write words and draw pictures to describe it.

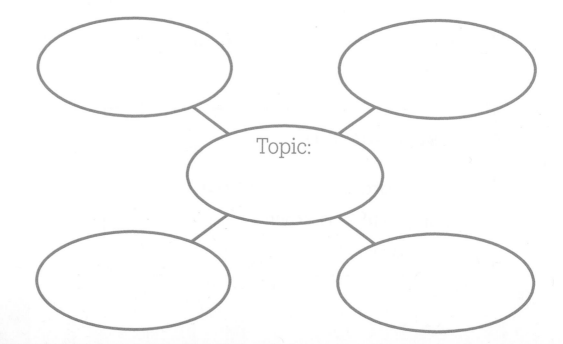

Topic:

52

WRITE Now write sentences to describe the desert land or desert creature. Remember to:

- Be sure each sentence tells about your topic.

- Use words to describe colors, sizes, how things feel, and other details.

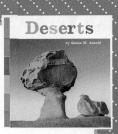
Deserts
by Quinn M. Arnold

Responses may vary.

Independent Close Reading

Have children close read and annotate "How an Island Is Made" on their own during small-group or independent work time. As needed, **use the Scaffolded Support notes** that follow to guide children who need additional help.

Scaffolded Support

As needed, remind children to:

- reread, look at the illustrations, ask questions, and think about what they already know to help them figure out things in the text they do not understand.

- use evidence from the text and pictures to figure out the central idea that the author wants to share.

DOK 2

Prepare to Read

GENRE STUDY **Informational text** is nonfiction. It gives facts about a topic.

MAKE A PREDICTION Preview **How an Island Is Made**. First, there is a volcano. Then, there is an island! What do you think you will learn?

I will learn how a
volcano makes an
island.

SET A PURPOSE Read to find out one way that islands are made. Find out if your prediction is right. If not, make a new prediction as you read.

54

How an Island Is Made

READ What happens to the lava from the volcano?

Islands have water all around them. How is an island made? One way is from a volcano on the bottom of the sea. Hot lava rises up out of the volcano. The water makes the lava cold. This turns it into rock.

Close Reading Tip

Circle words you don't know. Then figure them out.

CHECK MY UNDERSTANDING

What could you do to help yourself if you didn't understand this part of the text?

Look at the photo.
Reread the words.

Scaffolded Support

As needed, remind children to:

- reread the text and look at the pictures to find details that can help them answer the question.
- look at the other words in the sentence and the illustrations to help them figure out the meaning of unknown words.

DOK 2

55

Close Reading Tip

Put a ? by the parts you have questions about.

READ <u>Underline</u> important things that happen after the lava comes out.

More and more lava comes out of the volcano. The pile of rock gets bigger. It gets so big that it comes up out of the water. A new island is made!

After a long time, plants will grow on the land. Birds and other animals will live here, too. Their home will be this island that was once just a volcano on the bottom of the sea.

CHECK MY UNDERSTANDING

What main thing, or central idea, is this text about?

A new island can be made by a volcano under the sea.

56

Cite Text Evidence

WRITE ABOUT IT Write a story to tell your classmates about a day you spend on the new island. What is it like? Use describing words. Draw it on another sheet of paper.

Responses will vary but should be a story that is about the island.

57

Scaffolded Support

As needed, remind children that describing words tell how things look, sound, feel, smell, and taste.

DOK 2

READ FOR UNDERSTANDING

Introduce the Text

- **Read aloud** and discuss the information about the genre.
- **Guide children** to set a purpose for reading to practice summarizing.
- **Provide information** about the background topic, Recycle to Make Art.
- **Tell children** to look for and think about the Power Words as they read.

Prepare to Read

GENRE STUDY **Procedural texts** tell how to do or make something. Look for:

- directions to follow
- steps that show order
- pictures that show what the final project will look like

POWER WORDS

edges

trace

SET A PURPOSE Read to understand the most important ideas. Look for details in the words and pictures to help you. **Summarize** by telling the important ideas in your own words.

Build Background: Recycle to Make Art

58

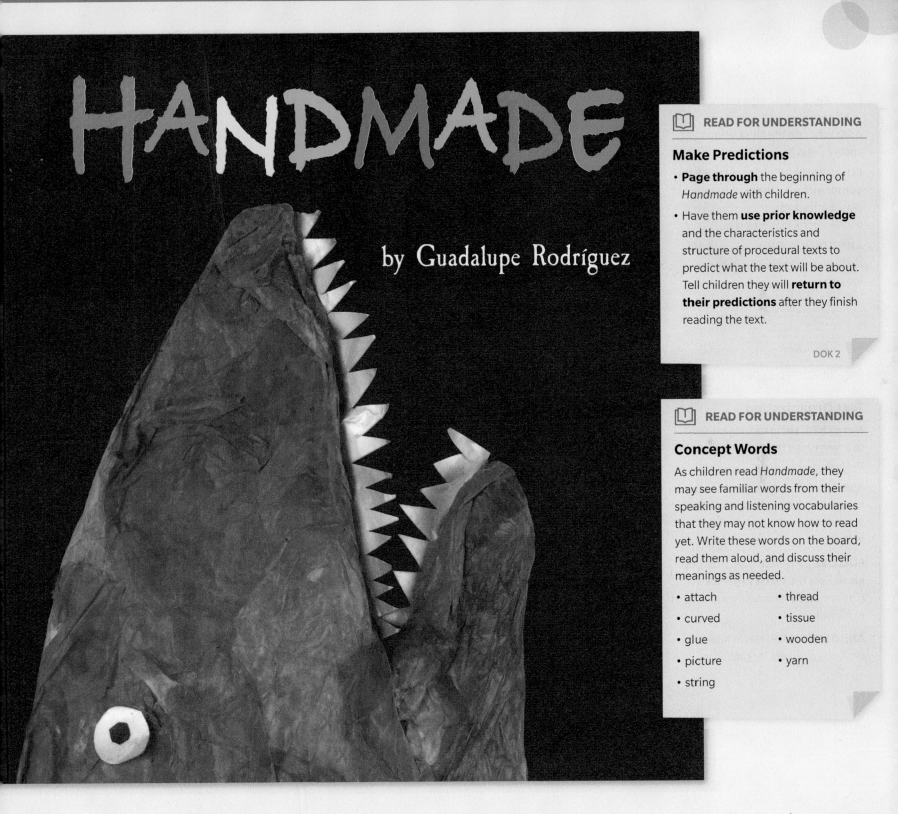

HANDMADE

by Guadalupe Rodríguez

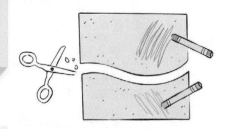
LANDSCAPE
WITH AN ANIMAL

1 On thick paper, draw a curved line. Cut. Color one part the color of the sky. Color the other one like grass or the ocean.

2 Put together the two parts by gluing only the ends. The center part stays open.

60

3 Get another piece of thick paper. Draw and color an animal. Then cut it out. Cut a strip of thick paper. Glue the end of the strip to the back of the animal. Let it dry.

4 Then put the strip through the open part of the landscape. Attach it with a paper fastener. Make your animal walk along the landscape by moving the strip back and forth.

READ FOR UNDERSTANDING

Summarize

MODEL SUMMARIZING

💬 **THINK ALOUD** *I can pause here to summarize what I am reading. What are the most important ideas? I use the words and pictures to help me tell them in my own words. To make a flying fish, I first have to cut out a shape from paper. Then I can color the eyes and body to make it look like a fish.*

DOK 2

🔍 **TARGETED CLOSE READ**

Text Organization

Have children reread pages 62–63 to analyze how the author organizes the text.

ASK: What does the author want you to learn from reading this text? *(how to make animals using different materials)*

FOLLOW-UP: How does the author organize the information to help you understand this? *(in steps that tell what to do first, next, and last)*

ANNOTATION TIP: Have children circle the numbers for each step.

DOK 3

FLYING
FISH

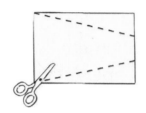

1 On a large sheet of paper, draw two lines like in the picture. Cut.

2 Color the eyes and the body. Glue the edges together.

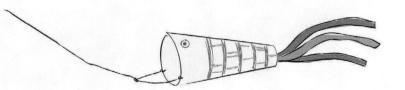

3 Tie a string to both sides of the mouth to make a loop. Tie on a long string to pull. Glue on strips of paper to make the tail.

📖 **READ FOR UNDERSTANDING**

Summarize

ASK: What do you learn about on pages 62–63? *(how to make a flying fish)*

FOLLOW-UP: What are the most important ideas? *(I can make a flying fish by cutting, coloring, and gluing a fish shape out of paper, and then attaching a string to it so that it can fly like a kite.)*

ANNOTATION TIP: Have children circle the action words in each step that tell what they need to do to make a flying fish.

DOK 2

📖 **READ FOR UNDERSTANDING**

ASK: What does the photo show that the words do not tell about? *(Possible response: how to fly the kite)*

FOLLOW-UP: Why do you think the author included the photo? *(Possible response: to show, instead of tell, how to fly the kite)*

DOK 2

Quick Teach Words

As needed to support comprehension, briefly explain the meaning of *half* in this context.

- To fold something in *half* means to fold it into two equal parts.

Phonics/Decoding in Context

Have children point to the word *thread*. Review that the letters *ea* can stand for the short vowel sound /ĕ/. **Model blending** the sounds in the word: /th/ /r/ /ĕ/ /d/, *thread*. Have children repeat.

Wrap Up

Revisit the predictions children made before reading. Have them confirm or correct their predictions using evidence from the text and pictures.

DOK 2

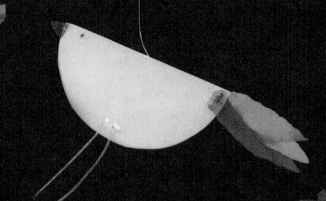

PAPER
BIRDS

1 Use a plate to trace a circle on paper. Cut the circle, and then fold it in half.

2 Draw and cut feathers and a beak out of tissue paper. Glue them on. Then draw an eye on each side of the paper. Get two wooden sticks for the legs. Glue them on.

3 Use thread or yarn to hang up the bird and . . . it'll be ready to fly!

64

Turn and Talk

Use details from **Handmade** to answer these questions with a partner.

1. Summarize What do you make in each project and how can it be used?

2. Tell the steps for making one of the projects. Use your own words.

Talking Tip

Ask a question if you are not sure about your partner's ideas.

What do you mean by _____?

Academic Discussion

Use the TURN AND TALK routine.
Remind children to use agreed-upon rules for discussion, such as listening carefully to their partners and asking questions to clear up any confusion.

Possible responses:

1. *You can make an animal in a landscape and use the animal like a puppet. You can make a flying fish and use it like a kite. You can also make birds and use them as a mobile.* DOK 2

2. *First, you cut a paper circle and fold it in half. Next, you make feathers and a beak out of tissue paper. Then you draw the eyes and glue sticks on for the legs. Last, you attach thread or yarn to make the bird fly.* DOK 2

65

READ
Together

Write a Letter

PROMPT Pick one of the projects from **Handmade**. Write a letter to tell someone you know how to make it. Use details from **Handmade** to help you explain the steps.

PLAN First, list materials the person will need, like paper. Write about the steps.

> First

> Next

> Last

Write About Reading
- **Read aloud** the prompt.
- **Lead a discussion** in which children summarize the instructions for each project. Tell them to use text evidence in the discussion.
- Then read aloud the Plan section. Have children use ideas from the discussion in their lists and steps.

DOK 2

WRITE Now write a letter to the person. Explain the steps for making the project. Remember to:

HANDMADE
by Guadalupe Rodríguez

- Tell all the materials that are needed.

- Explain the steps in order.

Responses may
vary.

Write About Reading

- **Read aloud** the Write section.

- **Encourage children** to use numbers and/or the sequence words *first, next,* and *last* in their explanations. Remind children to also include all the materials in their letters.

DOK 3

67

Independent Close Reading

Have children close read and annotate "Be a Bird Helper" on their own during small-group or independent work time. As needed, **use the Scaffolded Support notes** that follow to guide children who need additional help.

Scaffolded Support

As needed, remind children that:

- they can use their own words to summarize the most important ideas in the text.

- authors sometimes help them understand a topic by explaining the steps they need to follow in order.

DOK 3

Prepare to Read

GENRE STUDY **Procedural texts** tell how to do or make something.

MAKE A PREDICTION Preview **Be a Bird Helper**. Look at the text features, like the numbers, pictures, and headings, to help you predict. What do you think you will learn?

I will learn how to make a bird feeder.

SET A PURPOSE Read to find out how to help birds and to see if your prediction is right. If not, use the text features to help you make a new prediction as you read.

Be a Bird Helper

READ Why do birds need our help? <u>Underline</u> words that tell.

You Can Help!

Some animals need our help. We can be kind to these animals. Sometimes birds need help in the winter. They cannot find very many things to eat. You can help them get food. Make a bird feeder!

Close Reading Tip

Is your prediction right so far? If not, look at the text features to help you make a new prediction.

CHECK MY UNDERSTANDING

In your own words, what is this part mostly about?

We can be kind by helping birds get food.

69

Scaffolded Support

As needed, remind children to:

• ask themselves, *Is this detail about why birds need our help important?* as they mark ideas in the text and pictures.

• use their own words to tell the important idea.

DOK 2

READ <u>Underline</u> words that show the order of the steps. After you read, use your own words to summarize how to make a bird feeder. Tell just the most important ideas.

How to Make a Bird Feeder

1 First, ask a grown-up to help you get a pinecone, birdseed, string, stick, and peanut butter or shortening.

2 Next, put shortening or peanut butter on the pinecone. Roll it in the seeds.

3 Then tie string to the pinecone.

4 Last, put the bird feeder in a tree. The birds will thank you by eating the seeds!

Close Reading Tip

Was your prediction about what you would learn correct? What were you right about? What was different?

Scaffolded Support

As needed, remind children that:

- clue words such as *first, next, then,* and *last* show the sequence of steps.

- thinking about why the author wrote the text will help them understand why the author organized the text the way he or she did.

DOK 2

CHECK MY UNDERSTANDING

How does the author make the steps easy to understand?

The author put the steps in order. They have numbers.

WRITE ABOUT IT Why do you think the author wrote **Be a Bird Helper**? Why do you think it is written the way it is, with steps? Use details from the text to help you explain your ideas.

I think the author likes birds and wants to help them. The author told us easy steps for making a bird feeder so we can help birds, too.

Scaffolded Support

As needed, guide children to revisit the headings and the important ideas they identified in the text to help them answer the question.

DOK 2

71

READ FOR UNDERSTANDING

Introduce the Text

- **Read aloud** and discuss the information about the genre.
- **Guide children** to set a purpose for reading to practice synthesizing important ideas.
- **Provide information** about the background topic, National Parks.
- **Tell children** to look for and think about the Power Words as they read.

Prepare to Read

GENRE STUDY **Informational text** is nonfiction. It gives facts about a topic. Look for:

- details and facts about a topic
- headings that stand out
- pictures with labels and captions

SET A PURPOSE Read to find out the most important ideas in each part. Then **synthesize**, or put the ideas together, to find out new things about the text and what it really means to you.

POWER WORDS
popular
fossils
rim
hike
affect

Build Background: National Parks

GRAND CANYON

by Sara Gilbert

WELCOME TO GRAND CANYON NATIONAL PARK

74

Wow! Look at all that rock! At the Grand Canyon, you can look deep into the earth. Some of the rocks are millions of years old.

75

The Grand Canyon is in Arizona.
It became a national park in 1919.
It is one of the most popular
national parks in the United States.

★ *Grand Canyon National Park*
▪ *Arizona*

Havasu Creek (below); Pinyon-Juniper Woodlands (next page)

76

ROCKS AND A RIVER

The Grand Canyon covers more than one million acres. Some of it is desert. Other parts have lots of trees. It is cooler in the forests.

77

The Colorado River runs through the Grand Canyon. It made the canyon walls. The rock layers are different colors. People can find fossils in the rock.

A fern fossil (right); Toroweap Overlook (below)

78

CANYON CREATURES

More than 500 kinds of animals and birds live here. The endangered California condor is one of them. Condors are the biggest birds in North America.

TARGETED CLOSE READ

Content-Area Words

Have children reread page 79 to determine the meaning of the word *condor*.

ASK: What questions could you ask to figure out what a condor is? *(Possible response: What clues can I find in the text and photo?)*

FOLLOW-UP: How would you answer your questions? *(The text says that condors are big birds and the photo shows a big bird flying.)*

ANNOTATION TIP: Have children underline the clues in the text and circle the clues in the photo that helped them figure out what *condor* means.

DOK 2

READ FOR UNDERSTANDING

Quick Teach Words

As needed to support comprehension, briefly explain the meaning of *endangered* in this context.

• If an animal is *endangered*, it is very rare and it could stop existing.

79

There are about 2,000 kinds of plants in the park. A few are found only in the Grand Canyon. They do not grow anywhere else.

A cactus (right); a white fir tree (below)

BEAUTIFUL VIEWS

Almost 5 million people visit in a year. You can ride a bus around the rim. You can hike down into the canyon. You can even raft on the Colorado River.

81

It can get very hot in the canyon. Drink lots of water. Look out for wild animals like mountain lions, too. Do not try to feed them!

A mountain lion (below)
Park visitors can see across the canyon for miles. (next page)

📖 **READ FOR UNDERSTANDING**

ASK: Why does the author include this advice about visiting the park?
(to let the reader know that the park can be a dangerous place)

DOK 2

82

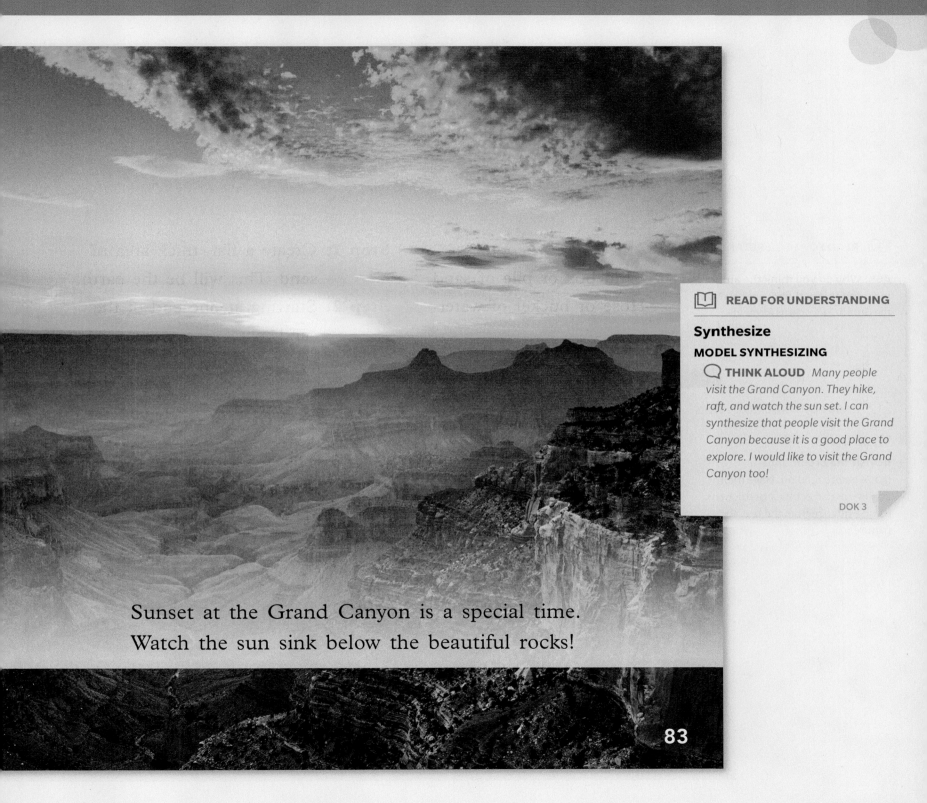

Sunset at the Grand Canyon is a special time.
Watch the sun sink below the beautiful rocks!

READ FOR UNDERSTANDING

Synthesize

MODEL SYNTHESIZING

THINK ALOUD *Many people visit the Grand Canyon. They hike, raft, and watch the sun set. I can synthesize that people visit the Grand Canyon because it is a good place to explore. I would like to visit the Grand Canyon too!*

DOK 3

83

ACTIVITY
CANYON CREATION

📖 **READ FOR UNDERSTANDING**

ASK: Why do you think the author included this activity? *(to show how the Grand Canyon was formed)*

DOK 2

📖 **READ FOR UNDERSTANDING**

Wrap Up

Revisit the predictions children made before reading. Have them confirm or correct their predictions using evidence from the text and pictures.

DOK 2

Materials needed:

Sand box or pile of sand

Hose or bucket of water

Step 1: Create a flat, thick area of sand. This will be the earth.

Step 2: Starting at one end of the sand, pour some water on it to make a river. What happens to the sand as the river runs through it?

Step 3: Add more water. Pour some of it quickly and some of it slowly. How does the speed affect what happens to the sand? Does the path of the river change? What happens to the walls around it?

Turn and Talk

GRAND CANYON
by Sara Gilbert

Use details from **Grand Canyon** to answer these questions with a partner.

1. **Synthesize** What are the most important ideas you learned? What makes the Grand Canyon seem special to you?

2. Reread the activity on page 84. Describe what you think will happen to the sand.

Listening Tip

Listen carefully. Make connections. How is what your partner says like other things you know?

85

READ Together

Write a Poem

PROMPT Write a poem about the Grand Canyon. Use details from **Grand Canyon** to describe things in an interesting way.

PLAN Write words that describe the Grand Canyon or something that lives there. Add rhyming words and words about the topic.

Write About Reading

- **Read aloud** the prompt.
- **Lead a discussion** in which children share their ideas about what the Grand Canyon is like. Tell children to use text evidence to support their ideas.
- Then read aloud the Plan section. Have children use ideas from the discussion in their charts.

DOK 2

Describing Words	Rhyming Words	Topic Words
huge	hot – lot – spot	fossils

WRITE Now write a poem to describe the Grand Canyon or something that lives there. Make the poem fun to say and hear! Then recite it for your classmates. You can:

- Use rhyming words and topic words.

- Repeat sounds and words, like **red red rocks**.

Responses may vary.

Write About Reading

- **Read aloud** the Write section.
- **Encourage children** to reread their poems and think about other words they can add to make them more interesting, such as rhyming words, repeated words, or words with repeated sounds.

DOK 3

87

88

Independent Close Reading

Have children close read and annotate "Grand Canyon Fossils" on their own during small-group or independent work time. As needed, **use the Scaffolded Support notes** that follow to guide children who need additional help.

Scaffolded Support

As needed, remind children to:

- identify the important ideas as they read and think about what those ideas mean to them.
- ask themselves questions and look for context clues to figure out the meaning of science words and phrases.

DOK 3

Prepare to Read

GENRE STUDY **Informational text** is nonfiction. It gives facts about a topic.

MAKE A PREDICTION Preview **Grand Canyon Fossils**. Fossils are what is left of living things from long ago. What do you think you will learn?

I will learn about kinds of fossils at the Grand Canyon.

SET A PURPOSE Read to find out about fossils in the Grand Canyon.

Grand Canyon Fossils

READ What is a fossil like? <u>Underline</u> words that tell.

Take a hike in the Grand Canyon and you just may find a fossil! As you walk, look around. You will see all kinds of rocks. Look closer! You see what looks like a shell in the rock. It is very old. You just found a fossil of an animal that lived long ago! ▶

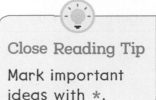

Close Reading Tip

Mark important ideas with *.

CHECK MY UNDERSTANDING

Where can you look for fossils in the Grand Canyon?

You can look in the rocks.

89

READ What kinds of fossils can you find? <u>Underline</u> them. What are the most important ideas you learn about fossils?

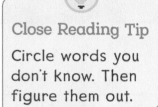

Close Reading Tip

Circle words you don't know. Then figure them out.

Shells are not the only fossils in the Grand Canyon. Long ago, this land was under the water. That's why we can find fossils of sea animals here, like **trilobites**. They look like bugs! You can find fossils of fish, coral, and sea sponges, too.

Plant fossils are also found in the Grand Canyon. Leaves, ferns, and small pine trees all left their prints in the rocks for us to find!

CHECK MY UNDERSTANDING

Use details in the words and photo to describe a **trilobite**.

It is a sea animal from long ago. It looks like a bug.

90

WRITE ABOUT IT Think about the important ideas from **Grand Canyon Fossils**. What do you think you can learn from looking at fossils? Write sentences to explain your ideas.

I can learn what animals and plants looked like long ago. I can find out how they are the same or different from ones that live today.

Scaffolded Support

As needed, guide children to make connections between important ideas they learned and what they mean to them.

DOK 2

91

READ
Together

📖 **VIEW FOR UNDERSTANDING**

Introduce the Video

- **Read aloud** and discuss the information about the genre.
- **Guide children** to set a purpose for viewing to practice identifying the central idea.
- Provide information about the background topic, The Water Cycle.

Prepare to View

GENRE STUDY **Songs** are words set to music. We can sing them out loud. Listen for:

- what the song is about
- the tune, or how the song sounds
- words or lines that are repeated

SET A PURPOSE Watch the video to find out the main message, or **central idea**, it shares about water. Look and listen for important details that help you understand it.

Build Background: The Water Cycle

92

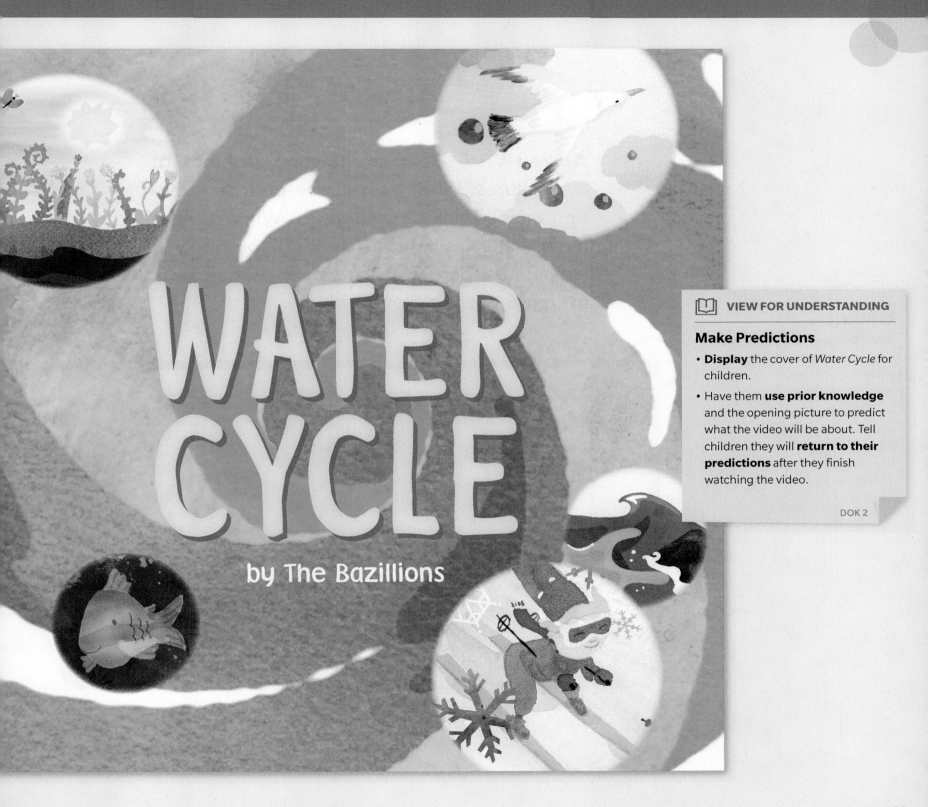

WATER CYCLE

by The Bazillions

📖 VIEW FOR UNDERSTANDING

Make Predictions

- **Display** the cover of *Water Cycle* for children.
- Have them **use prior knowledge** and the opening picture to predict what the video will be about. Tell children they will **return to their predictions** after they finish watching the video.

DOK 2

As You View Listen to the song and look at the pictures. What do you see and hear over and over? Think as you watch. What is the main thing this video is showing you about water? Use details in the words and pictures to figure out this central idea.

📖 **VIEW FOR UNDERSTANDING**

Central Idea

ASK: What does the author want you to learn from watching this video? (what the water cycle is and why it is important)

FOLLOW-UP: What evidence lets you know? (The video shows how the water cycle happens over and over again, and then tells about things we wouldn't have if the water cycle didn't happen.)

DOK 3

94

Use details from **Water Cycle** to answer these questions with a partner.

1. Central Idea What is the main thing, or central idea, the video explains about the water cycle?

2. Tell how clouds are an important part of the water cycle.

Talking Tip

Speak loudly enough. Do not speak too fast or too slow.

I think _____ because _____.

95

**Revisit the
Essential Question**

• **Read aloud** the Essential Question.

• **Remind children** that in this
module, they read different texts
about the natural world that can
help them answer the question.

• **Have children** choose one of the
activities to show what they learned
in this module.

Recycled Art

• **Prompt children** to think about
different materials they can recycle
and use to make their pictures, such
as yarn, milk cartons, or paper cups.

• **Guide children** to think of ways
they care for the earth at school and
at home.

DOK 2

Let's Wrap Up!

(?) **Essential Question**

How do things in nature change?

Pick one of these activities to show what
you have learned about the topic.

1. Recycled Art

Nature changes the Earth and
so do people! Make a
picture of the Earth using
scraps of paper and
other things that can be
recycled. Write about
ways we can take care
of our Earth.

96

2. Season Expert

Pick a season. Draw and label a picture of a place you know in that season. Tell a partner about the weather and other changes that happen in that season.

Word Challenge

Can you use the word cycle to help explain what happens?

Season Expert

- **Guide children** to think about the things they can and can't do during the season they chose, and to share that information with their partners.
- **Encourage them** to use the Big Idea Word *cycle* in their explanation.

DOK 2

Brainstorm and Plan

Have children use the My Notes space to jot down ideas for their chosen activity. Remind them to refer back to their notes as they complete the activity.

My Notes

97

Introduce the Topic

- **Read aloud** the module title, *Tell Me a Story.*

- **Tell children** that in this module they will be reading texts about the topic of what stories teach us.

- **Have children** share prior knowledge about the topic or word associations for what stories teach us. Record their ideas in a web.

Discuss the Quotation

- **Read aloud** the Hispanic proverb.

- **Lead a discussion** in which children try to explain the quote in their own words. Explain the meaning, as needed: *Sometimes it takes hard work to learn something new, but once you learn it, you will never forget it.*

ASK: When have you worked hard to learn something? *(Accept reasonable responses.)*

MODULE
8

Tell Me a Story

"Lessons learned when you are young last a lifetime."

—Hispanic Proverb

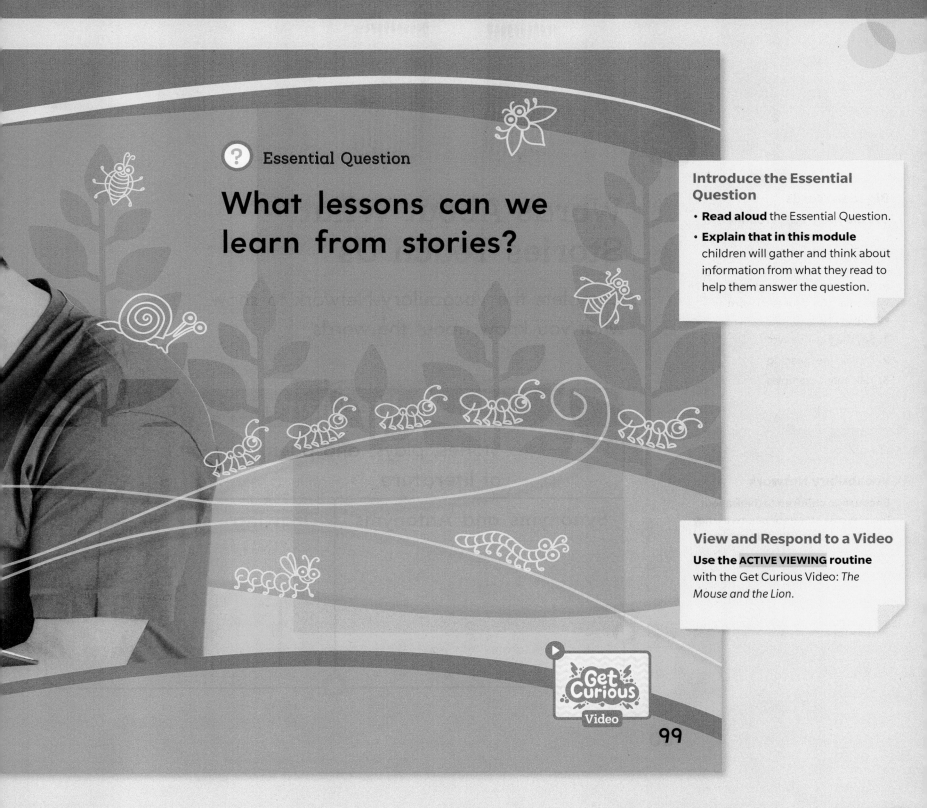

? Essential Question

What lessons can we learn from stories?

Introduce the Essential Question

- **Read aloud** the Essential Question.
- **Explain that in this module** children will gather and think about information from what they read to help them answer the question.

View and Respond to a Video

Use the ACTIVE VIEWING routine with the Get Curious Video: *The Mouse and the Lion*.

Get Curious Video

99

Words About What Stories Teach Us

Complete the Vocabulary Network to show what you know about the words.

literature
Meaning: Stories, plays, and poems are all kinds of **literature**.

Synonyms and Antonyms	Drawing

100

entertain

Meaning: When you want to **entertain** people, you could act, sing, or dance.

Synonyms and Antonyms	Drawing

amuse

Meaning: If you **amuse** people, you make them smile or laugh.

Synonyms and Antonyms	Drawing

Vocabulary Network

- **As children complete** the activity for *entertain*, prompt them to think of songs, dances, or dramas they are familiar with.

- **Ask children** to think about things they think are funny or that make them laugh as they complete the activity for *amuse*.

101

Follow the Story Path

What are the parts of a story? Follow the path to find out.

CHARACTERS

Characters are the people or animals in a story.

SETTING

The **setting** is where and when the story happens.

BEGINNING

The events in the **beginning** tell what the **problem** is. The problem is what goes wrong.

102

MIDDLE

The events in the **middle** tell how the characters try to solve the problem.

END

The events at the **end** tell the **resolution**, or how the problem is solved.

Now follow the path again. Tell your own version of the story of the two goats! Use the pictures for help.

READ FOR UNDERSTANDING

Text Features

ASK: What do you learn from this diagram? *(the parts of a story in order)*

FOLLOW-UP: What do the arrows tell you? *(where to start to read the diagram and where to end)*

DOK 2

READ FOR UNDERSTANDING

Text Features

ASK: Why does the author use bold text? *(to call attention to important words in the text)*

FOLLOW-UP: How are the different color and bold words different? *(The bold words are not on the path.)*

DOK 2

103

READ FOR UNDERSTANDING

Introduce the Text

- **Read aloud** and discuss the information about the genre.
- **Guide children** to set a purpose for reading to practice creating mental images.
- **Provide information** about the author and illustrator, David Ezra Stein.
- **Tell children** to look for and think about the Power Words as they read.

Prepare to Read

GENRE STUDY **Fantasy** stories have made-up events that could not really happen. Look for:

- animal characters that act like people
- short tales within this story
- a problem and a resolution

SET A PURPOSE Make pictures in your mind as you read. Words that tell how things look, sound, feel, taste, or smell and words about feelings help you **create mental images**.

POWER WORDS

interrupt

follow

involved

supposed

relaxing

warn

Meet David Ezra Stein.

104

INTERRUPTING CHICKEN

This book is called Interrupting Chicken, right, Papa?

Yes. Now, please don't interrupt the story!

by David Ezra Stein

📖 **READ FOR UNDERSTANDING**

Make Predictions

- **Page through** the beginning of *Interrupting Chicken* with children.

- Have them **use prior knowledge** and the illustrations to predict what the story will be about. Tell children they will **return to their predictions** after they finish reading the story.

DOK 2

 READ FOR UNDERSTANDING

Concept Words

As children read *Interrupting Chicken*, they may see familiar words from their speaking and listening vocabularies that they may not know how to read yet. Write these words on the board, read them aloud, and discuss their meanings as needed.

- Chicken Little
- Ducky Lucky
- Goosey Loosey
- Gretel
- Hansel
- Henny Penny
- Little Red Riding Hood
- Papa
- wolf

It was bedtime for the little red chicken.

READ FOR UNDERSTANDING

ASK: Who are the characters in the story? *(Papa and little chicken)*

FOLLOW-UP: Which details in the text and illustrations tell you this? *(The illustrations show an adult chicken and a young chicken. The text tells what Papa and little chicken say to each other.)*

DOK 2

"Okay, my little chicken," said Papa. "Are you all ready to go to sleep?"

"Yes, Papa! But you forgot something."

"What's that?" asked Papa.

"A bedtime story!"

106

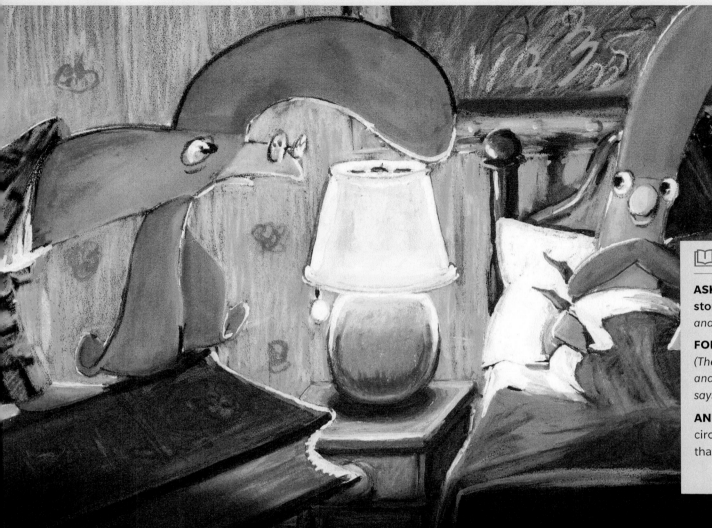

READ FOR UNDERSTANDING

ASK: When and where does this story take place? *(at night, in Papa and little chicken's home)*

FOLLOW-UP: How do you know? *(The picture shows Papa wearing a robe and little chicken is in her bed. The text says it's bedtime.)*

ANNOTATION TIP: Have children circle the words on pages 106–107 that tell about the setting.

DOK 2

"All right," said Papa. "I'll read one of your favorites. And of course you are not going to *interrupt* the story tonight, are you?"

"Oh no, Papa. I'll be good."

107

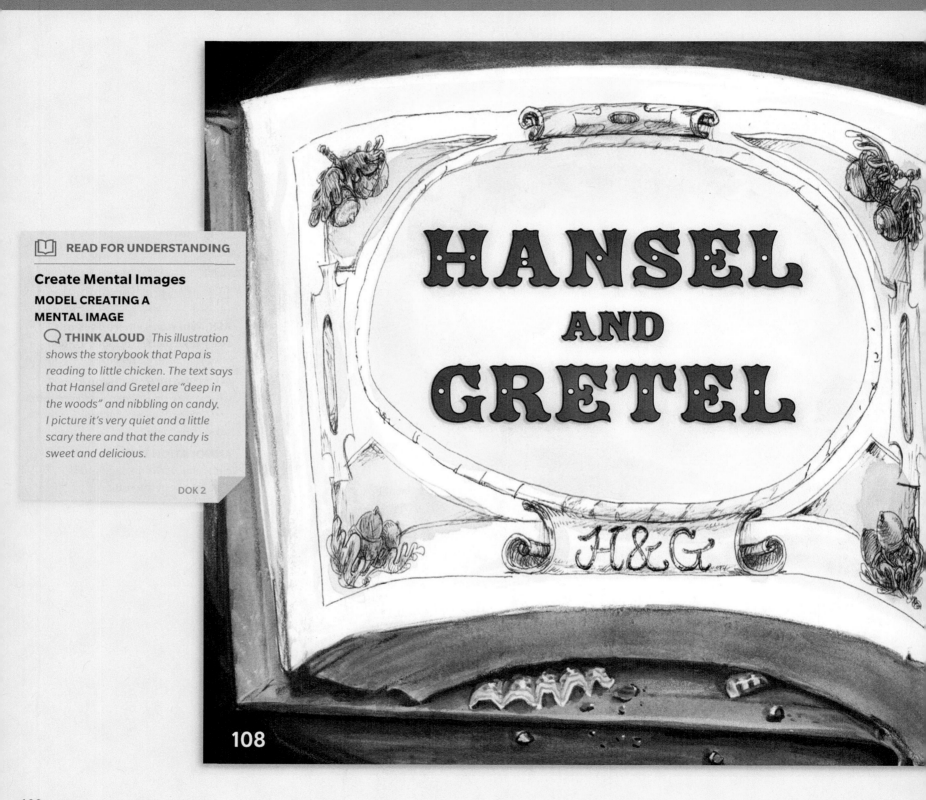

Create Mental Images

MODEL CREATING A MENTAL IMAGE

THINK ALOUD *This illustration shows the storybook that Papa is reading to little chicken. The text says that Hansel and Gretel are "deep in the woods" and nibbling on candy. I picture it's very quiet and a little scary there and that the candy is sweet and delicious.*

DOK 2

HANSEL AND GRETEL

H & G

108

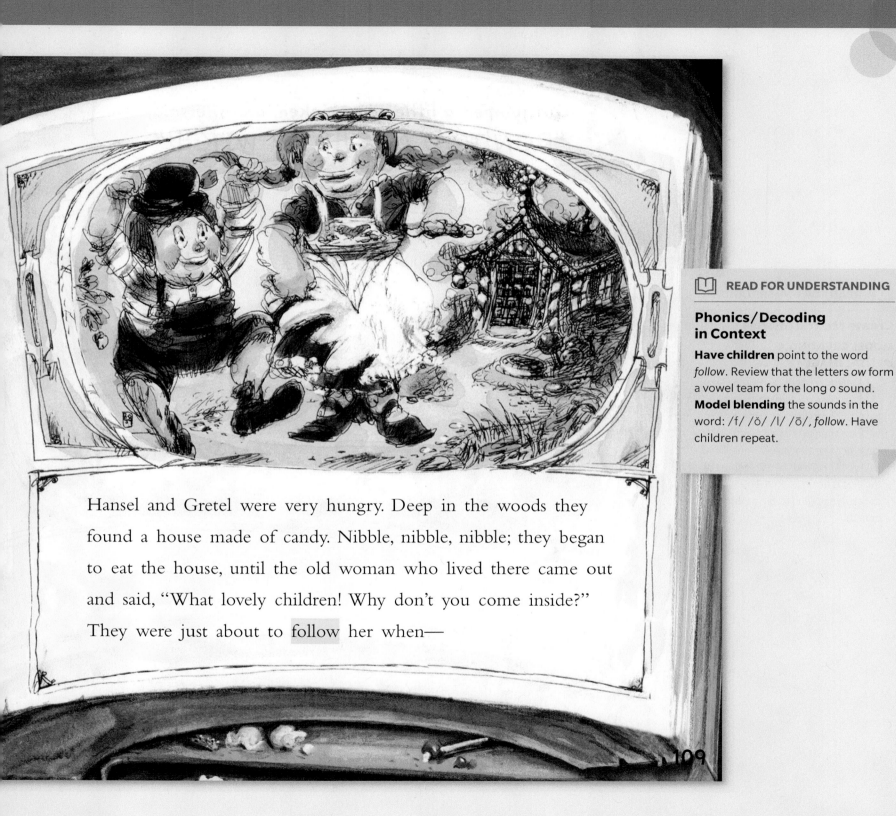

READ FOR UNDERSTANDING

Phonics/Decoding in Context

Have children point to the word *follow*. Review that the letters *ow* form a vowel team for the long *o* sound.
Model blending the sounds in the word: /f/ /ŏ/ /l/ /ō/, *follow*. Have children repeat.

Hansel and Gretel were very hungry. Deep in the woods they found a house made of candy. Nibble, nibble, nibble; they began to eat the house, until the old woman who lived there came out and said, "What lovely children! Why don't you come inside?" They were just about to follow her when—

Create Mental Images

MODEL CREATING A MENTAL IMAGE

THINK ALOUD *Here I see little chicken inside the storybook! I know that it was really quiet in the woods, but now that little chicken is there, it looks like she's yelling at Hansel and Gretel. I know that because some of the words are in capital letters and the sentences end in exclamation points.*

DOK 2

So Hansel and Gretel didn't.
THE END!

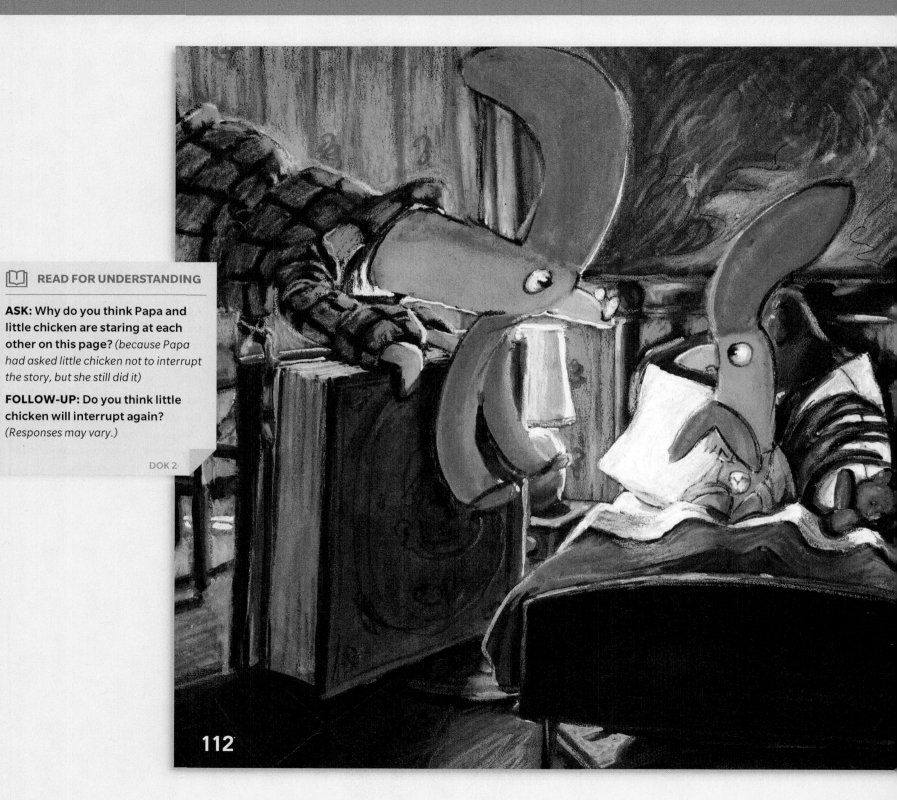

112

"Chicken."

"Yes, Papa?"

"You interrupted the story. Try not to get so involved."

"I'm sorry, Papa. But she really was a witch."

"Well, you're supposed to be relaxing so you can fall asleep."

"Let's try another story. I'll be good!"

Notice & Note

Words of the Wiser

- **Remind children** that when a wise character shares advice, they should stop to notice and note. Explain that this can help them understand or create a mental image about something important that is happening in the story.

- **Have children** explain why they might use this strategy on page 113. (*Papa tells little chicken that she shouldn't get so involved in the story. She interrupts and does not relax and go to sleep.*)

ANNOTATION TIP: Have children underline the sentence or sentences that tell the advice Papa gives to little chicken.

- **Remind them** of the Anchor Question: **What's the life lesson and how might it affect little chicken?** (*The lesson is that getting excited during a bedtime story will not help you go to sleep. Little chicken might try to stay quiet and listen so she can go to sleep.*)

DOK 3

113

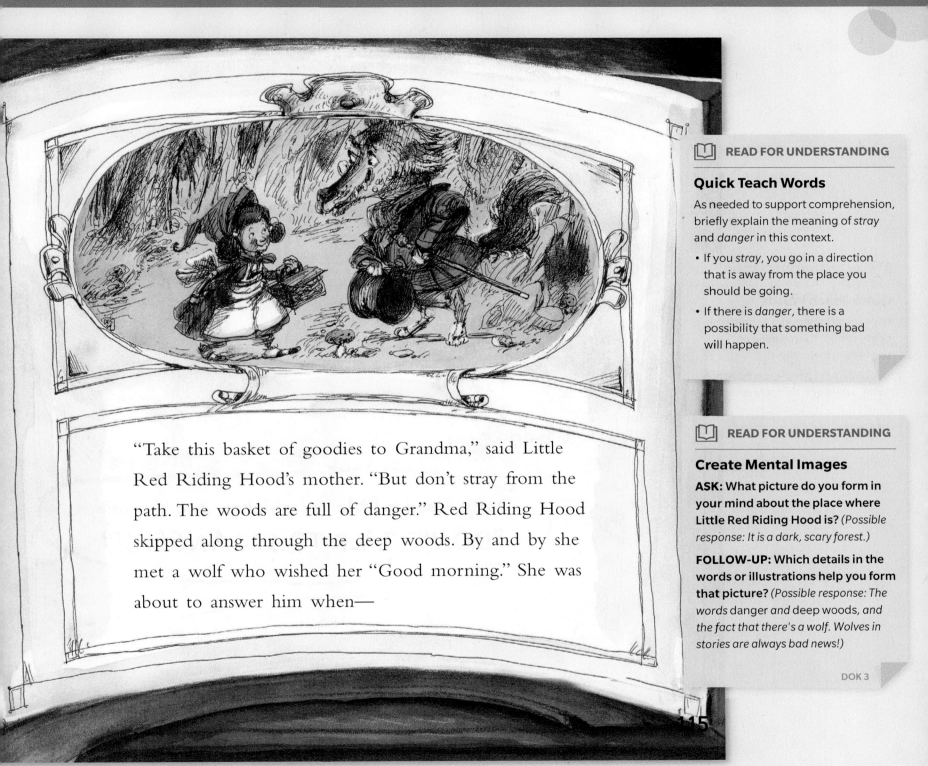

"Take this basket of goodies to Grandma," said Little Red Riding Hood's mother. "But don't stray from the path. The woods are full of danger." Red Riding Hood skipped along through the deep woods. By and by she met a wolf who wished her "Good morning." She was about to answer him when—

READ FOR UNDERSTANDING

Quick Teach Words

As needed to support comprehension, briefly explain the meaning of *stray* and *danger* in this context.

- If you *stray*, you go in a direction that is away from the place you should be going.
- If there is *danger*, there is a possibility that something bad will happen.

READ FOR UNDERSTANDING

Create Mental Images

ASK: What picture do you form in your mind about the place where Little Red Riding Hood is? (*Possible response: It is a dark, scary forest.*)

FOLLOW-UP: Which details in the words or illustrations help you form that picture? (*Possible response: The words* danger *and* deep woods, *and the fact that there's a wolf. Wolves in stories are always bad news!*)

DOK 3

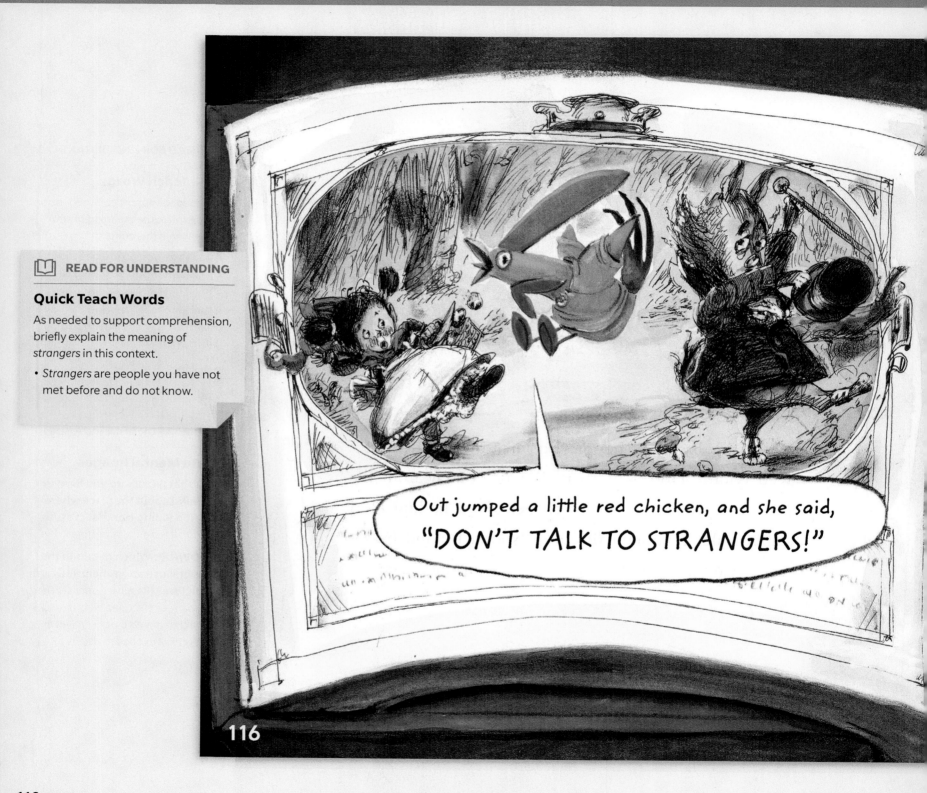

Quick Teach Words

As needed to support comprehension, briefly explain the meaning of *strangers* in this context.

- *Strangers* are people you have not met before and do not know.

Out jumped a little red chicken, and she said,
"DON'T TALK TO STRANGERS!"

116

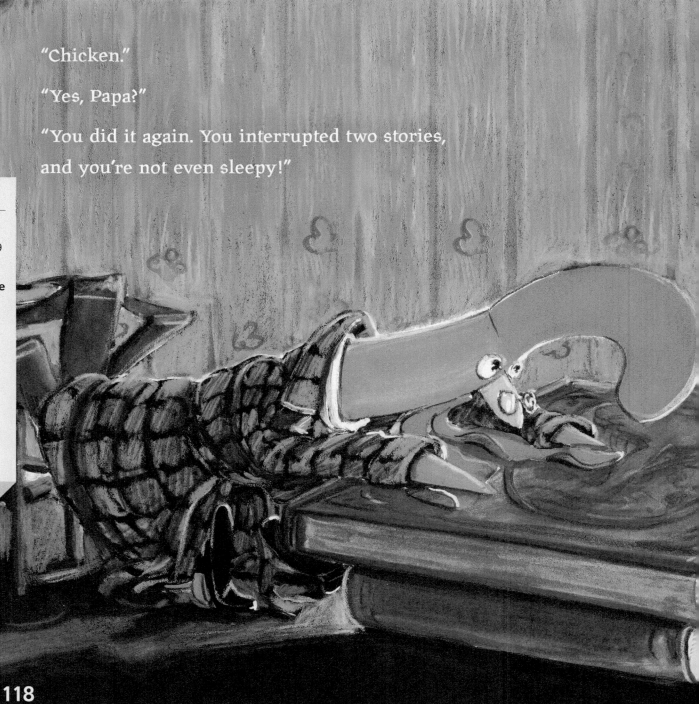

"Chicken."

"Yes, Papa?"

"You did it again. You interrupted two stories, and you're not even sleepy!"

TARGETED CLOSE READ

Characters

Have children reread pages 118–119 to analyze a story character.

ASK: How does Papa feel when little chicken keeps interrupting?
(Possible response: He feels frustrated and tired.)

FOLLOW-UP: How do you know?
(Papa says, "You did it again." He is bending over and looks tired.)

ANNOTATION TIP: Have children underline the words Papa says that help them know why Papa feels the way he does.

DOK 2

118

"I know, Papa! I'm sorry. But he was a *mean* old wolf."

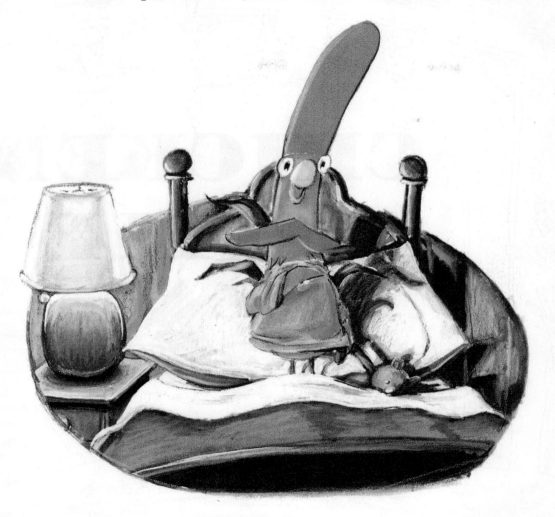

📖 **READ FOR UNDERSTANDING**

ASK: Is little chicken sleepy? (*She is not. She is standing on her bed. Some of her sentences have exclamation marks, so that means she is excited.*)

FOLLOW-UP: Do you think Papa will read her another story? Which one? (*Accept reasonable responses.*)

ANNOTATION TIP: Have children circle the exclamation marks on page 119 that help them know how little chicken is feeling.

DOK 2

"Yes. Now get back into bed."

"Okay, Papa. Let's try one more *little* story, and I'll be good!"

119

READ FOR UNDERSTANDING

ASK: How are little chicken and Chicken Little similar? (*Possible responses: They are both chickens; they both tell others about danger.*)

FOLLOW-UP: How are they different? (*Possible response: Little chicken interrupts stories because she does not like what happens in them; Chicken Little is about to warn everyone that the sky was falling.*)

DOK 2

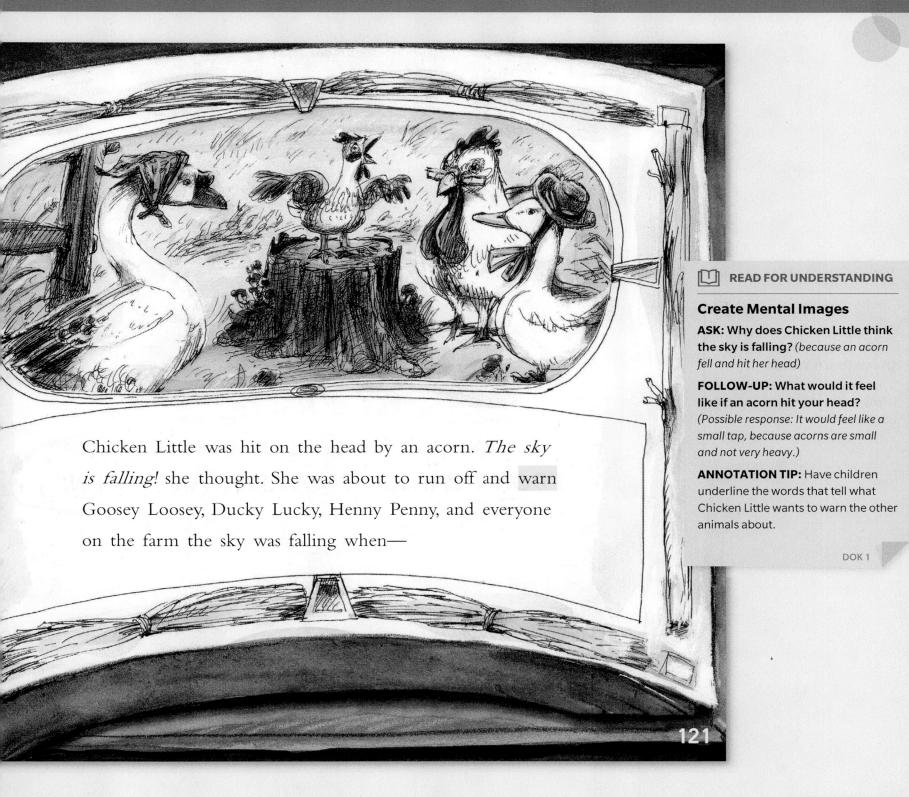

Chicken Little was hit on the head by an acorn. *The sky is falling!* she thought. She was about to run off and warn Goosey Loosey, Ducky Lucky, Henny Penny, and everyone on the farm the sky was falling when—

📖 **READ FOR UNDERSTANDING**

Create Mental Images

ASK: Why does Chicken Little think the sky is falling? *(because an acorn fell and hit her head)*

FOLLOW-UP: What would it feel like if an acorn hit your head? *(Possible response: It would feel like a small tap, because acorns are small and not very heavy.)*

ANNOTATION TIP: Have children underline the words that tell what Chicken Little wants to warn the other animals about.

DOK 1

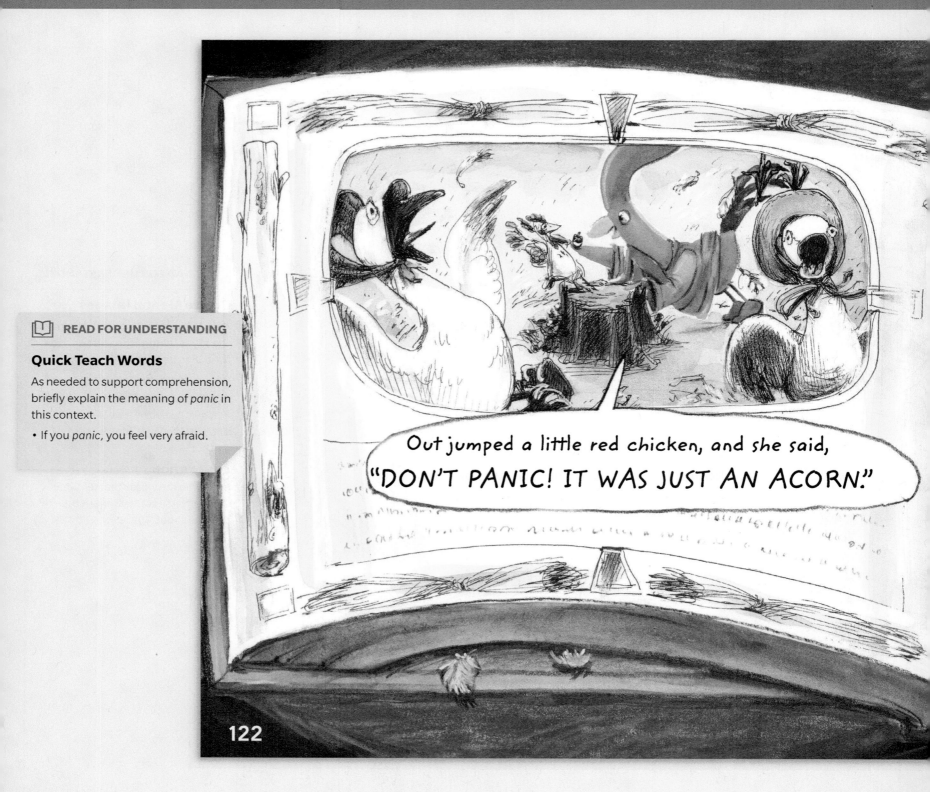

READ FOR UNDERSTANDING

Quick Teach Words

As needed to support comprehension, briefly explain the meaning of *panic* in this context.

• If you *panic*, you feel very afraid.

So Chicken Little didn't.
THE END!

123

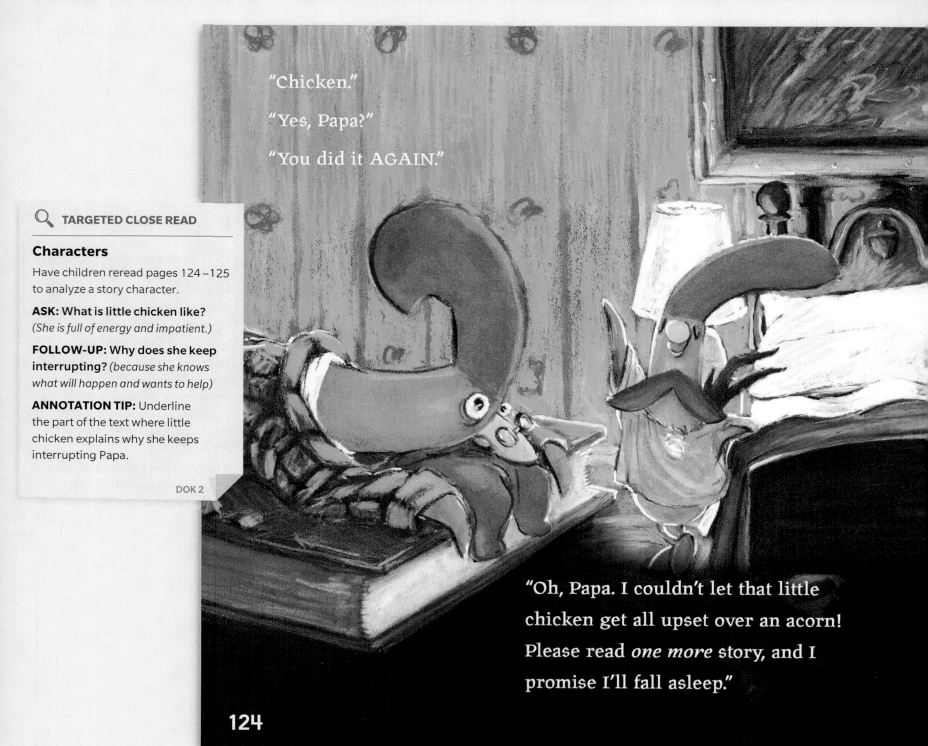

"Chicken."

"Yes, Papa?"

"You did it AGAIN."

"Oh, Papa. I couldn't let that little chicken get all upset over an acorn! Please read *one more* story, and I promise I'll fall asleep."

TARGETED CLOSE READ

Characters

Have children reread pages 124–125 to analyze a story character.

ASK: What is little chicken like? *(She is full of energy and impatient.)*

FOLLOW-UP: Why does she keep interrupting? *(because she knows what will happen and wants to help)*

ANNOTATION TIP: Underline the part of the text where little chicken explains why she keeps interrupting Papa.

DOK 2

124

"But Chicken," said Papa,
"we are out of stories."

"Oh no, Papa. I can't go
to sleep without a story!"

READ FOR UNDERSTANDING

ASK: What do you think little chicken's story will be about?
(*Responses will vary.*)

DOK 2

"Then," said Papa, yawning, "why don't you tell *me* a story?"

"*Me* tell a story?" said the little red chicken. "Okay, Papa!
Here we go! Um . . ."

125

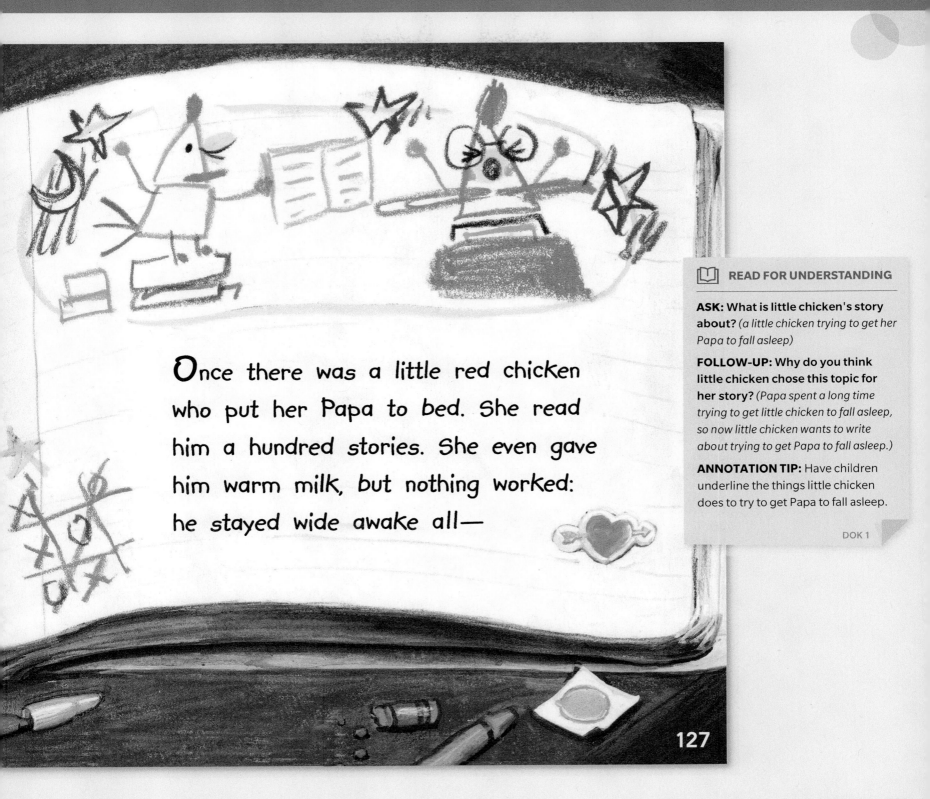

Once there was a little red chicken who put her Papa to bed. She read him a hundred stories. She even gave him warm milk, but nothing worked: he stayed wide awake all—

127

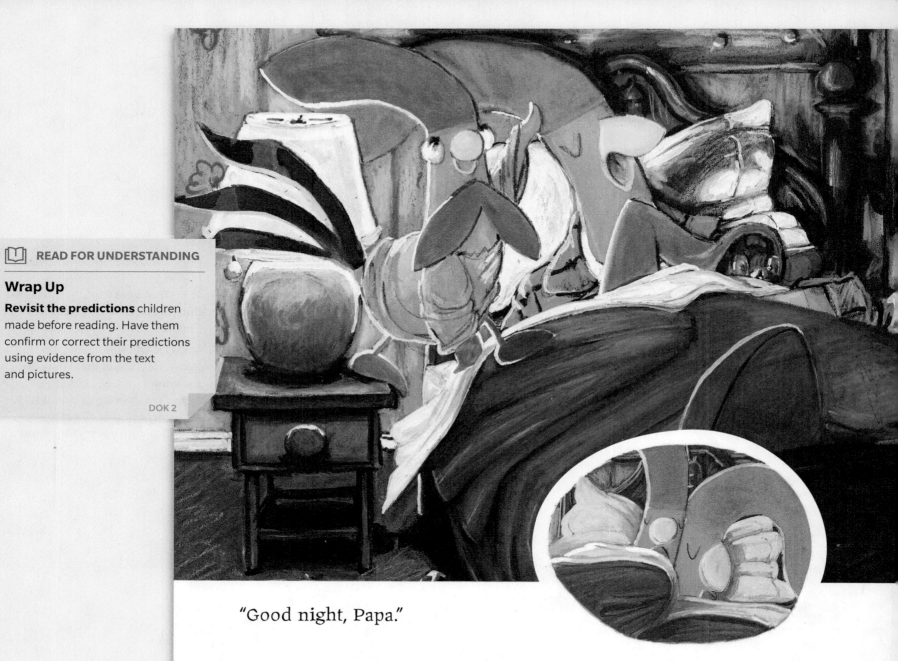

READ FOR UNDERSTANDING

Wrap Up

Revisit the predictions children made before reading. Have them confirm or correct their predictions using evidence from the text and pictures.

DOK 2

"Good night, Papa."

THE END

130

Turn and Talk

Use details from **Interrupting Chicken** to answer these questions with a partner.

1. **Create Mental Images** What pictures did you create in your mind when Chicken interrupted each story? Which words helped you create those pictures?

2. Tell why the ending of the story is funny.

Talking Tip

Wait for your turn to speak. Explain your ideas and feelings clearly.

I think _____ because _____.

Academic Discussion

Use the TURN AND TALK routine. Remind children to follow agreed-upon rules for discussion, such as taking turns and explaining their ideas and feelings carefully.

Possible responses:

1. *I created a mental image of little chicken jumping up out of bed. The words "out jumped" helped me create those pictures.* DOK 1

2. *The ending is funny because Papa fell right asleep in the middle of the first story, unlike little chicken!* DOK 2

131

Write a Story

PROMPT Look back at the bedtime story about Chicken Little in **Interrupting Chicken**. Tell that story in your own way.

PLAN First, write your ideas for the beginning, middle, and end of the story.

WRITE Now write your story about Chicken Little. Use your own words. Remember to:

- Tell the beginning, middle, and end.

- Use words like **first**, **next**, and **last** to show the order of the events that happen.

Responses may vary.

Prepare to Read

GENRE STUDY **Fantasy** stories have made-up events that could not really happen.

MAKE A PREDICTION Preview **Hansel and Gretel Two**. Think about how a fantasy has make-believe events. What do you think will happen?

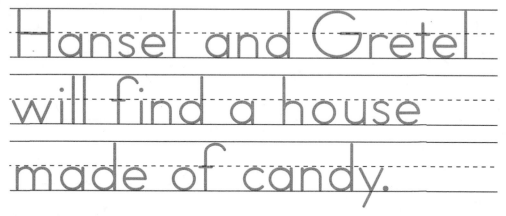

Hansel and Gretel will find a house made of candy.

SET A PURPOSE Read to find out what Hansel and Gretel do and to see if your prediction is right. If not, make a new prediction.

134

Hansel and Gretel Two

READ Describe what Hansel and Gretel are doing. Tell why.

One day, we were hiking in the forest.

"Hansel, look! That little house over there has shiny red and yellow candy all over it," said Gretel. "Yum! I'm hungry."

"I'm hungry, too! Let's take a nibble," I said. Just then, out jumped a little chicken!

Close Reading Tip

Is your prediction right so far? If not, think about the genre and make a new prediction.

Scaffolded Support

As needed, remind children that:

- describing words are words that tell what things look like. These words can help them form a mental image of the house.

- using details from the text and illustrations can help them understand what the characters are doing and why.

- the events in stories happen in an order that makes sense.

DOK 2

CHECK MY UNDERSTANDING

Which words help you picture what the house is like?

little; shiny red and yellow candy

135

Close Reading Tip

Write C when you make a connection.

Scaffolded Support

As needed, remind children that:

- paying attention to the things the characters say and do can help them understand what they are like.

- they can use clues in the text and illustrations to help them understand why characters do the things they do.

DOK 2

READ Why do the children invite the chicken to their house? <u>Underline</u> words that tell.

"DON'T EAT THAT! IT'S NOT GOOD FOR YOUR TEETH!" the little chicken yelled.

We decided that this funny chicken was just trying to help us and so must be nice.

"Do you want to come to our house to play?" I asked the little chicken.

"Is it made of candy?" she asked with a grin. And we all hiked off together!

CHECK MY UNDERSTANDING

Describe what Hansel and Gretel are like. How do you know?

They are friendly and brave. They make friends with the chicken.

136

Cite Text Evidence

WRITE ABOUT IT How are the things that Hansel and Gretel do in this new story different from what they did in **Interrupting Chicken**? Write to explain.

Responses will vary but should compare characters' actions from the two stories.

137

Scaffolded Support

As needed, guide children to look back at Hansel and Gretel in *Interrupting Chicken*. Have them review what the characters in each story say and do.

DOK 3

📖 READ FOR UNDERSTANDING

Introduce the Text

• **Read aloud** and discuss the information about the genre.

• **Guide children** to set a purpose for reading to practice making connections.

• **Provide information** about the author, Lisa Campbell Ernst.

• **Tell children** to look for and think about the Power Words as they read.

Prepare to Read

GENRE STUDY **Dramas** are stories that are read and acted out. Look for:

• a setting where the story takes place

• dialogue, or what the characters say

• a narrator called the Storyteller

SET A PURPOSE As you read, **make connections** by finding ways that this text is like things in your life and other texts you have read. This will help you understand and remember the text.

POWER WORDS
storyteller
sly
boldly

Meet Lisa Campbell Ernst.

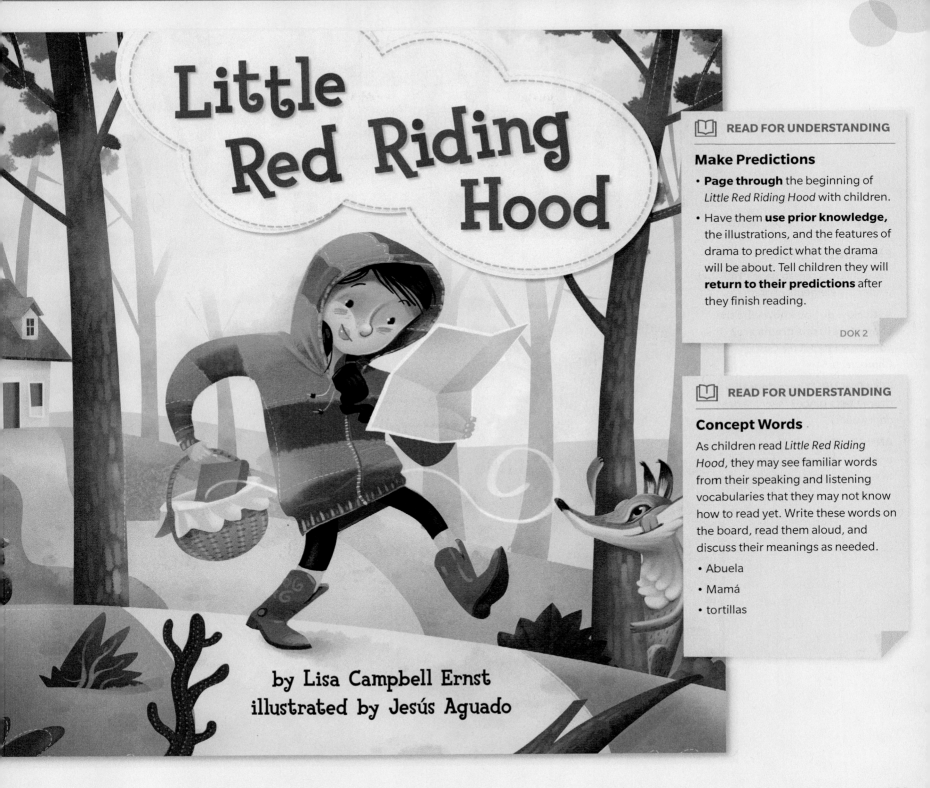

Little Red Riding Hood

by Lisa Campbell Ernst

illustrated by Jesús Aguado

Elements of Drama

Have children reread pages 140–141 to identify elements of drama.

ASK: How do you know who the characters in this drama are? (*their names are listed in the Cast of Characters*)

FOLLOW-UP: Where does this drama take place? (*near the deep, dark woods*)

ANNOTATION TIP: Have children underline the sentence that tells where the drama takes place.

DOK 2

Cast:

Storyteller

Little Red Riding Hood

Mamá

Coyote

Abuela

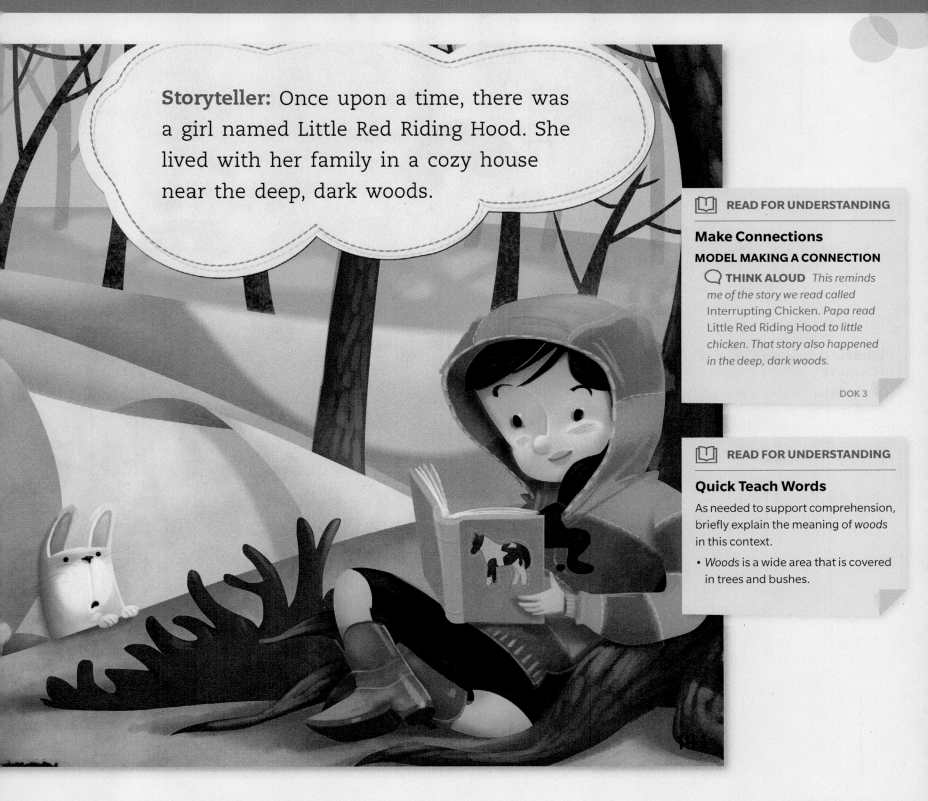

Storyteller: Once upon a time, there was a girl named Little Red Riding Hood. She lived with her family in a cozy house near the deep, dark woods.

**Phonics/Decoding
in Context**

Have children point to the word
right. Review that the letters *igh* stand
for the long *i* sound. Model blending
the sounds in the word: /r/ /ī/ /t/,
right. Have children repeat.

Mamá: Little Red Riding Hood, your grandmother
is sick. I'm making fresh, tasty tortillas. Will you
please take them to Abuela?

Little Red Riding Hood: Yahoo! Abuela loves
tortillas! I'll bring a book to read to her, too. I'll
leave right now.

142

Mamá: Slow down, dear! Here's a map that shows the path to Abuela's house. Stay on the path, and please be careful.

Little Red Riding Hood: This map shows that it's close by. I'll stay on the path. I'll be fine.

Map to Abuela's House

Notice & Note

Words of the Wiser

- **Remind children** that when a wise character shares advice, they should stop to notice and note. Explain that this can help them understand or make connections about something important that is happening in the story.

- **Have children** explain why they might use this strategy on page 143. (*Mamá tells Little Red Riding Hood to use the map and be careful when she's walking in the woods.*)

ANNOTATION TIP: Have children circle the dialogue where Mamá gives Little Red Riding Hood advice.

- **Remind them** of the Anchor Question: **What's the life lesson and how might it affect Little Red Riding Hood?** (*You should follow directions and stay on the path so you don't run into any trouble.*)

DOK 3

📖 READ FOR UNDERSTANDING

Quick Teach Words

As needed to support comprehension, briefly explain the meaning of *dear* in this context.

- You can use *dear* instead of saying the name of a person you love.

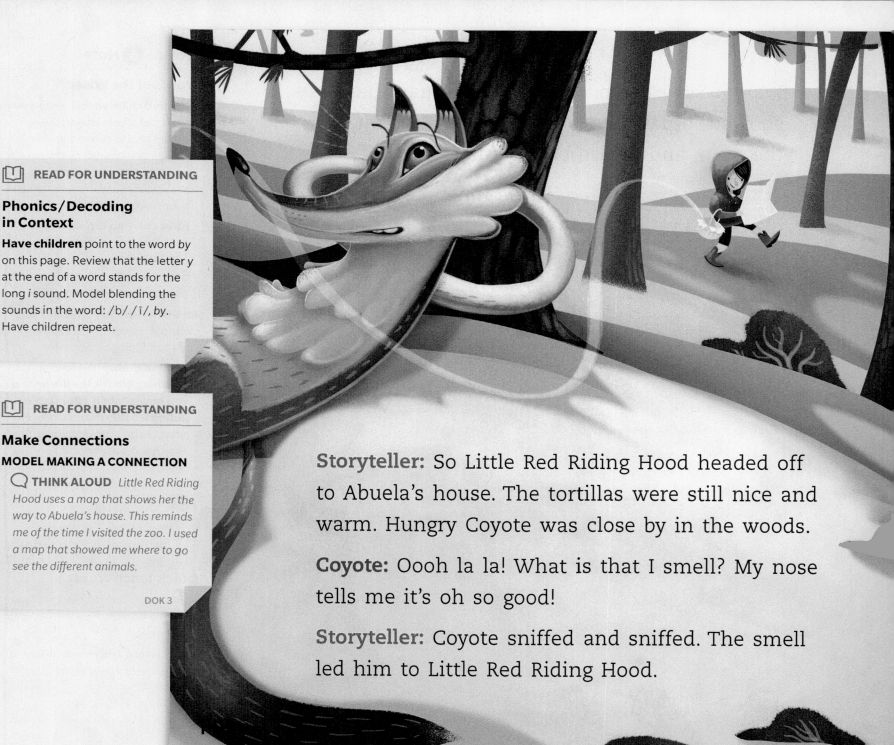

READ FOR UNDERSTANDING

Phonics/Decoding in Context

Have children point to the word *by* on this page. Review that the letter *y* at the end of a word stands for the long *i* sound. Model blending the sounds in the word: /b/ /ī/, *by*. Have children repeat.

READ FOR UNDERSTANDING

Make Connections

MODEL MAKING A CONNECTION

THINK ALOUD *Little Red Riding Hood uses a map that shows her the way to Abuela's house. This reminds me of the time I visited the zoo. I used a map that showed me where to go see the different animals.*

DOK 3

Storyteller: So Little Red Riding Hood headed off to Abuela's house. The tortillas were still nice and warm. Hungry Coyote was close by in the woods.

Coyote: Oooh la la! What is that I smell? My nose tells me it's oh so good!

Storyteller: Coyote sniffed and sniffed. The smell led him to Little Red Riding Hood.

Coyote: Well, hi there! Who are you, and where are you going on this fine day?

Little Red Riding Hood: I'm Little Red Riding Hood. I'm taking tortillas to my sick grandmother. This is my map. It shows me the way.

Storyteller: Hungry Coyote looked at the map and got a mean idea. He had a sly smile on his face.

📖 **READ FOR UNDERSTANDING**

Make Connections

ASK: How is this drama different from the story Papa reads in *Interrupting Chicken*? (*In this one, Little Red Riding Hood is talking to Coyote, and the story continues. In the story Papa reads, little chicken interrupts the story, so Little Red Riding Hood doesn't get a chance to talk to the wolf, and the story ends.*)

DOK 3

145

Coyote: Look at these nice flowers! Flowers might help your grandmother feel better. Why don't you pick some?

Little Red Riding Hood: Thanks for the idea! I'll pick some bright flowers for Abuela.

🔍 **TARGETED CLOSE READ**

Elements of Drama

Have children reread pages 146–147 to identify elements of drama.

ASK: Who is talking on these pages? *(Coyote, Little Red Riding Hood, and Storyteller)*

FOLLOW-UP: What do the words that Coyote says help you learn about him? *(He pretends to be kind to Little Red Riding Hood, but he is really just trying to trick her.)*

ANNOTATION TIP: Have children circle the sentences that help them understand that Coyote is trying to trick Little Red Riding Hood.

DOK 2

146

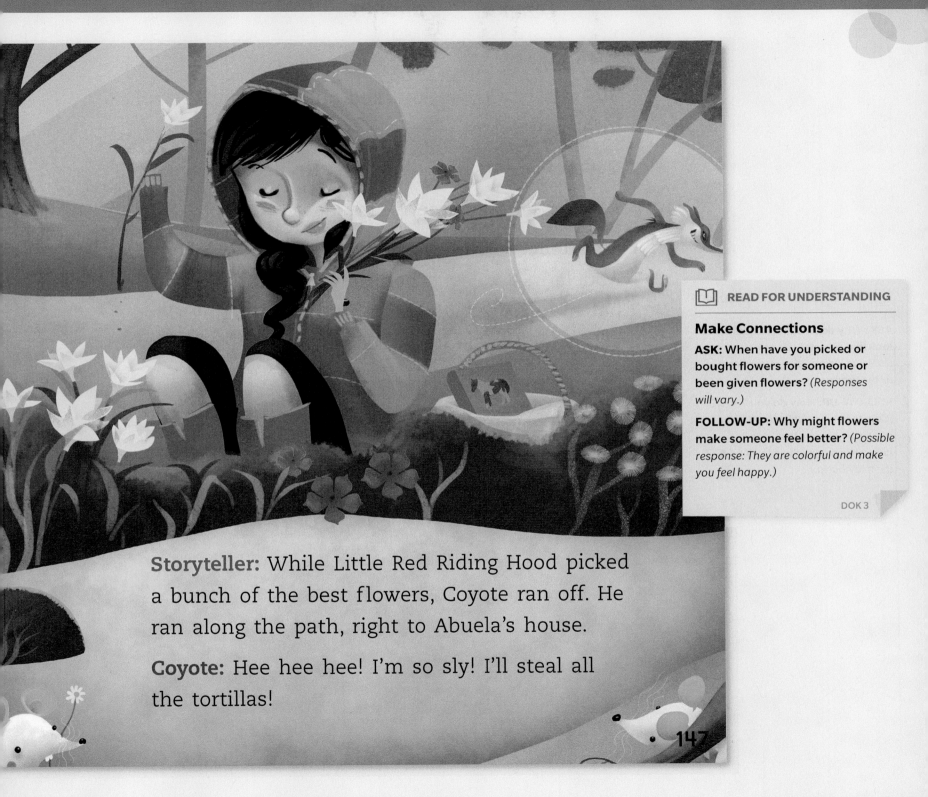

Make Connections

ASK: When have you picked or bought flowers for someone or been given flowers? *(Responses will vary.)*

FOLLOW-UP: Why might flowers make someone feel better? *(Possible response: They are colorful and make you feel happy.)*

DOK 3

Storyteller: While Little Red Riding Hood picked a bunch of the best flowers, Coyote ran off. He ran along the path, right to Abuela's house.

Coyote: Hee hee hee! I'm so sly! I'll steal all the tortillas!

147

Storyteller: Coyote knocked on the door. He spoke in a high voice.

Coyote: Hi, Abuela! It's me, Little Red Riding Hood!

Abuela: Please come in, my dear.

Storyteller: Coyote leaped in. He boldly locked Abuela in a closet. Then he put on a dress and hat to look like her. Soon, Little Red Riding Hood was outside. She knocked.

📖 **READ FOR UNDERSTANDING**

ASK: Why does Coyote dress up to look like Abuela? *(He wants to trick Little Red Riding Hood into giving him all the tortillas.)*

FOLLOW-UP: How do you know? *(Coyote said he wanted to steal the tortillas. He knows that Little Red Riding Hood is planning to give them to Abuela.)*

DOK 3

148

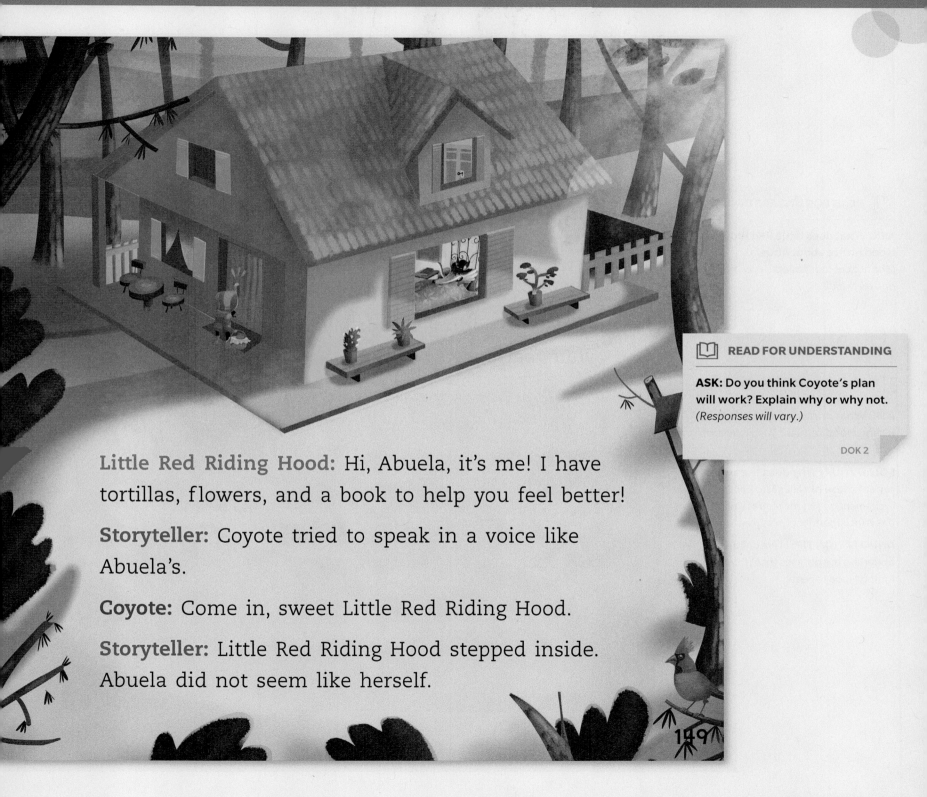

READ FOR UNDERSTANDING

ASK: Do you think Coyote's plan will work? Explain why or why not. *(Responses will vary.)*

DOK 2

Little Red Riding Hood: Hi, Abuela, it's me! I have tortillas, flowers, and a book to help you feel better!

Storyteller: Coyote tried to speak in a voice like Abuela's.

Coyote: Come in, sweet Little Red Riding Hood.

Storyteller: Little Red Riding Hood stepped inside. Abuela did not seem like herself.

Little Red Riding Hood: My, Abuela, your eyes are so big!

Coyote: So I can see you, my dear.

Little Red Riding Hood: My, Abuela, your ears are so big!

Coyote: So I can hear you read to me, my dear.

Little Red Riding Hood: My, Abuela, your teeth are so big!

📖 **READ FOR UNDERSTANDING**

ASK: What does Little Red Riding Hood notice about Abuela?
(She notices that Abuela's eyes, ears, and teeth look big.)

DOK 1

📖 **READ FOR UNDERSTANDING**

ASK: What phrases does Little Red Riding Hood repeat? *(My, Abuela; are so big!)*

FOLLOW-UP: Why does the author repeat these phrases? *(to build excitement and let the reader know that this is an important part of the story)*

ANNOTATION TIP: Have children underline the phrases that Little Red Riding Hood repeats.

DOK 3

150

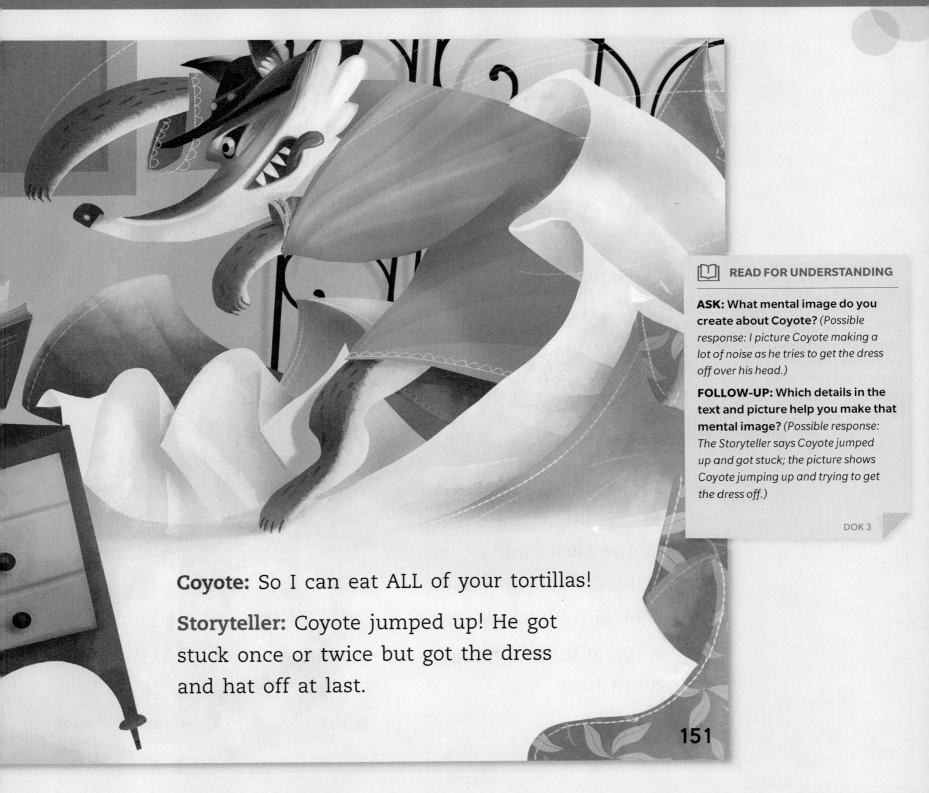

Coyote: So I can eat ALL of your tortillas!

Storyteller: Coyote jumped up! He got stuck once or twice but got the dress and hat off at last.

151

READ FOR UNDERSTANDING

ASK: How do Little Red Riding Hood and Abuela feel about Coyote being in Abuela's house? (*Possible response: They don't understand what he is doing there.*)

FOLLOW-UP: How do you know? (*Abuela asks "What's going on in here?" In the pictures, Little Red Riding Hood and Abuela look confused.*)

DOK 2

Storyteller: Just then, Little Red Riding Hood got a text message.

Little Red Riding Hood: Wait just a minute...

Storyteller: She read the message out loud.

Little Red Riding Hood: *I'm in the closet. Please let me out! Love, Abuela.*

Storyteller: Brave Little Red Riding Hood dashed to the closet and unlocked it. In a flash, Abuela jumped out.

Abuela: What's going on in here?

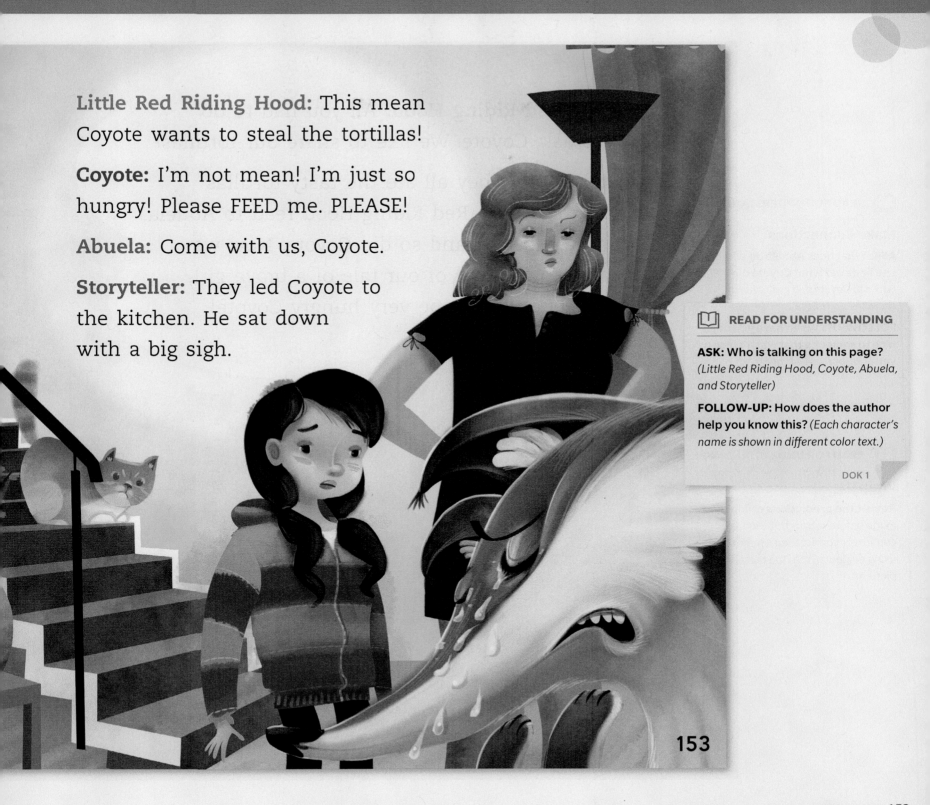

Little Red Riding Hood: This mean Coyote wants to steal the tortillas!

Coyote: I'm not mean! I'm just so hungry! Please FEED me. PLEASE!

Abuela: Come with us, Coyote.

Storyteller: They led Coyote to the kitchen. He sat down with a big sigh.

153

Little Red Riding Hood: All you had to do was ask, Coyote. We like to share our tortillas!

Storyteller: They all ate the tasty tortillas together. Little Red Riding Hood read to Abuela. She felt better, and so did Coyote. Now we come to the end of our tale of a brave girl, her Abuela, and one very hungry Coyote!

 READ FOR UNDERSTANDING

Make Connections

ASK: What does Abuela do when she finds out what Coyote did? *(She is nice to Coyote and invites him to share their tortillas.)*

FOLLOW-UP: When have you been nice to someone that wasn't nice to you? *(Responses will vary.)*

DOK 3

 READ FOR UNDERSTANDING

Wrap Up

Revisit the predictions children made before reading. Have them confirm or correct their predictions using evidence from the text and pictures.

DOK 2

Turn and Talk

Use details from **Little Red Riding Hood** to answer these questions with a partner.

1. **Make Connections** How is this story of Little Red Riding Hood like the one in **Interrupting Chicken**? How is it different?

2. Why does Little Red Riding Hood change the way she feels about Coyote during the story?

Listening Tip

Look at your partner. Listen politely and think about what your partner is saying.

155

Write a Drama

PROMPT Where will the characters from **Little Red Riding Hood** go next? Write a short drama to add on to the story.

PLAN First, draw a picture of what is happening in your new scene.

WRITE Now write your short drama. Tell what everyone says and does. Use another sheet of paper if you need to. Then share it with classmates. Tell them what things about your writing make it a drama. Remember to:

- Begin with a list of the **characters**.

- Name the place and describe this **setting**.

- Make the **dialogue** sound like real talking.

Responses may vary.

Write About Reading
- **Read aloud** the Write section.
- **Encourage children** to add describing words that tell more about the characters and setting. Have them add to the dialogue to make it sound like real people sound when they speak.

DOK 3

157

Prepare to Read

GENRE STUDY **Dramas** are stories that are read and acted out.

MAKE A PREDICTION Preview **Keep Trying**. A girl is trying to learn how to ride a bike. What do you think will happen?

She will fall down and then try again to ride the bike.

SET A PURPOSE Read to find out if the girl learns to ride her bike.

158

Keep Trying

READ Who is in this drama? <u>Underline</u> the characters' names.

Cast: **Narrator**   **June**   **Max**

Narrator: June is learning to ride a bike in the park. Her big brother is helping her.

June: I'll never learn how to ride this bike. I think I'm going to fall!

Max: Just keep trying, June! ▶

Close Reading Tip
Write C when you make a connection.

CHECK MY UNDERSTANDING

Describe the setting where the drama takes place.

The setting is a park with trees in a city.

159

Close Reading Tip

Put a ! by a surprising part.

READ What does the dialogue tell you about June?

Narrator: June didn't learn at first, but she didn't give up.

Max: You're getting better. You're almost ready to take off by yourself, June.

June: OK, Max, I'm ready. Let go!

Narrator: June started to fall! But she didn't. She learned an important lesson. If you can't do something at first, keep trying!

CHECK MY UNDERSTANDING

How are **Keep Trying** and **Little Red Riding Hood** alike?

Both have brave girl characters, a cast, a setting, and dialogue.

160

Cite Text Evidence

WRITE ABOUT IT How does June learn a lesson in **Keep Trying**? Use examples from the drama to explain your answer.

June tried and tried to ride her bike. She almost fell. But, she did not give up, and she learned to ride a bike.

Scaffolded Support

As needed, guide children to reread the story and review what happens first, next, and last to find out how June learns a lesson.

DOK 2

Prepare to Read

GENRE STUDY **Fables** have been told for many years and teach a lesson. Look for:

- animals that are characters
- how the pictures and words help you understand what happens

SET A PURPOSE Read to make smart guesses, or **inferences**, about things the author does not say. Use what you already know and clues in the text and pictures to help you.

POWER WORDS
labor
chirped
autumn

▶ **Meet Jerry Pinkney.**

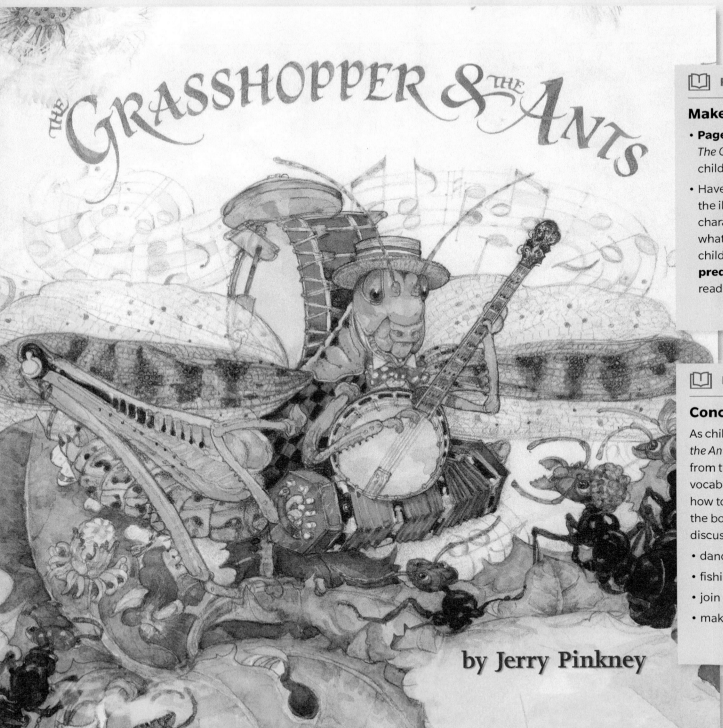

THE GRASSHOPPER & THE ANTS

by Jerry Pinkney

164

"Why work so hard?"
sang Grasshopper.
"It's spring and time to go fishing."

"No time to relax,"
said the Ants.

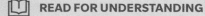

Quick Teach Words

As needed to support comprehension, briefly explain the meaning of *grasshopper* in this context.

- A *grasshopper* is an insect that has long legs it uses to jump. In this book, the word *grasshopper* starts with a capital letter. That means that the grasshopper's name is also Grasshopper.

Make Inferences

MODEL MAKING AN INFERENCE

🗨 **THINK ALOUD** *The pictures show the Ants working hard to gather food. The words say that there is no time to relax. I can use these clues to make an inference. I think the Ants need to gather food now so they have enough to eat later on.*

DOK 2

165

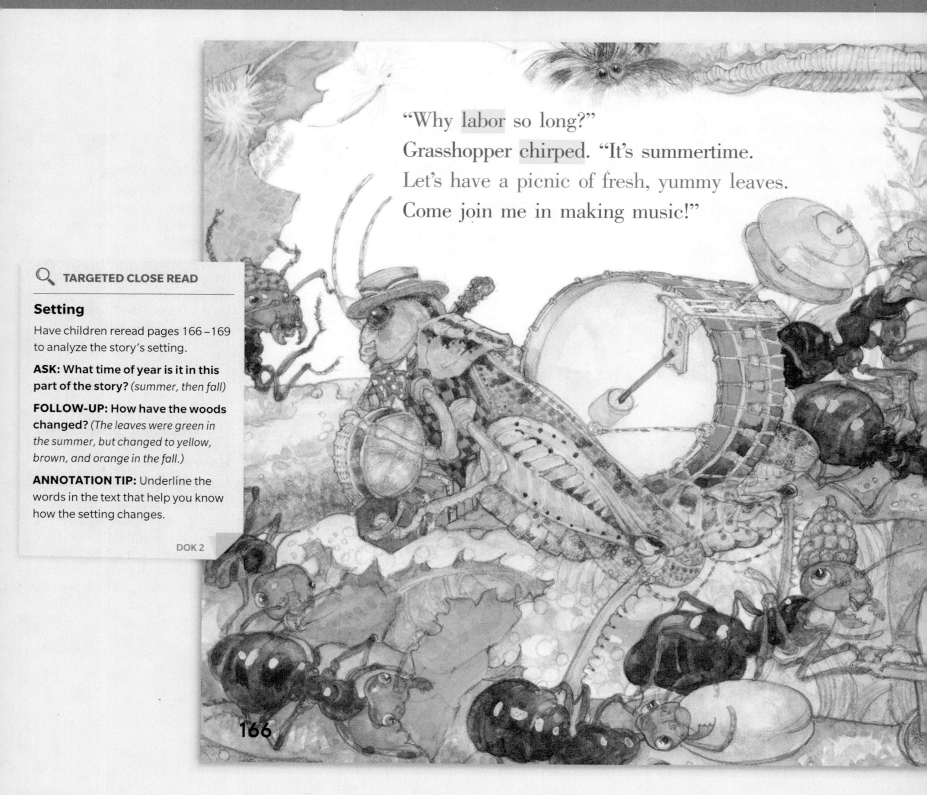

"Why labor so long?"
Grasshopper chirped. "It's summertime.
Let's have a picnic of fresh, yummy leaves.
Come join me in making music!"

🔍 **TARGETED CLOSE READ**

Setting

Have children reread pages 166–169 to analyze the story's setting.

ASK: What time of year is it in this part of the story? *(summer, then fall)*

FOLLOW-UP: How have the woods changed? *(The leaves were green in the summer, but changed to yellow, brown, and orange in the fall.)*

ANNOTATION TIP: Underline the words in the text that help you know how the setting changes.

DOK 2

166

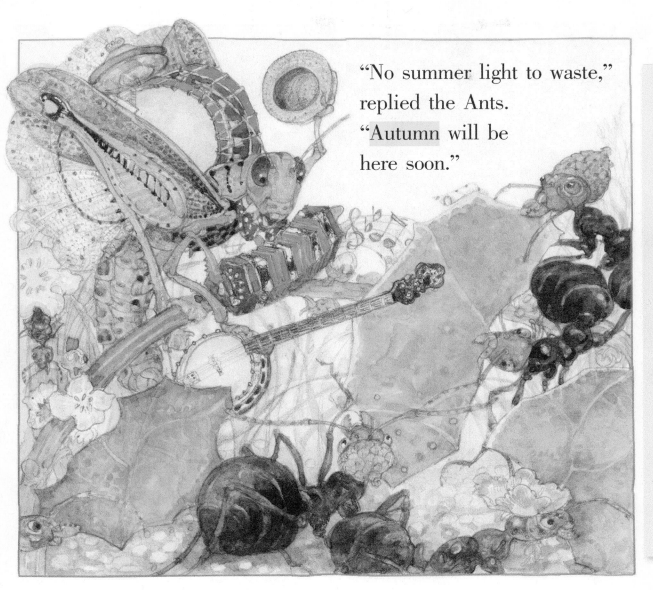

"No summer light to waste," replied the Ants. "Autumn will be here soon."

Notice & Note

Words of the Wiser

- **Remind children** that when a wise character shares advice, they should stop to notice and note. Explain that this is a clue that they should make inferences about something important that is happening in the story.

- **Have children** explain why they might use this strategy on page 167. (*The Ants tell Grasshopper that they can't waste time having fun because it will be cold soon.*)

ANNOTATION TIP: Have children underline the sentence or sentences that tell the advice the Ants give Grasshopper.

- **Remind them** of the Anchor Question: **What's the life lesson and how might it affect Grasshopper?** (*The lesson is that you should work hard and plan for the future instead of just having fun all the time.*)

DOK 3

READ FOR UNDERSTANDING

Quick Teach Words

As needed to support comprehension, briefly explain the meaning of *steady* in this context.

- If you do something in a *steady* way, you do it for a long time without stopping.

"Why toil so steady?" asked Grasshopper.
"It's fall and the world is a playground of leaves.
Oh, how their colors twirl and glide!
Come dance and sing!"

168

"Look at this wonderful mountain of leaves. Come play!"

📖 **READ FOR UNDERSTANDING**

Quick Teach Words

As needed to support comprehension, briefly explain the meaning of *mountain* in this context.

• A *mountain* of something is a very large amount of it.

169

🔍 **TARGETED CLOSE READ**

Setting

Have children reread page 170 to analyze the story's setting.

ASK: What are the woods like now? *(There are no leaves on the trees; it's cold and snowy.)*

FOLLOW-UP: How has the setting changed? *(The story begins in the spring, then it changes to summer, then autumn, and now it's winter.)*

DOK 2

"And oh, how I love the sparkle of first snow. Come see!"

170

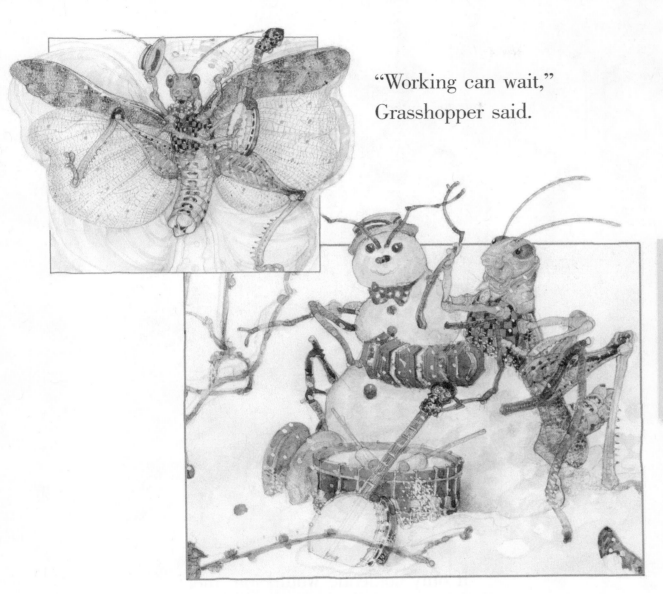

"Working can wait," Grasshopper said.

"Wintertime is for making snow angels and snow-hoppers."

171

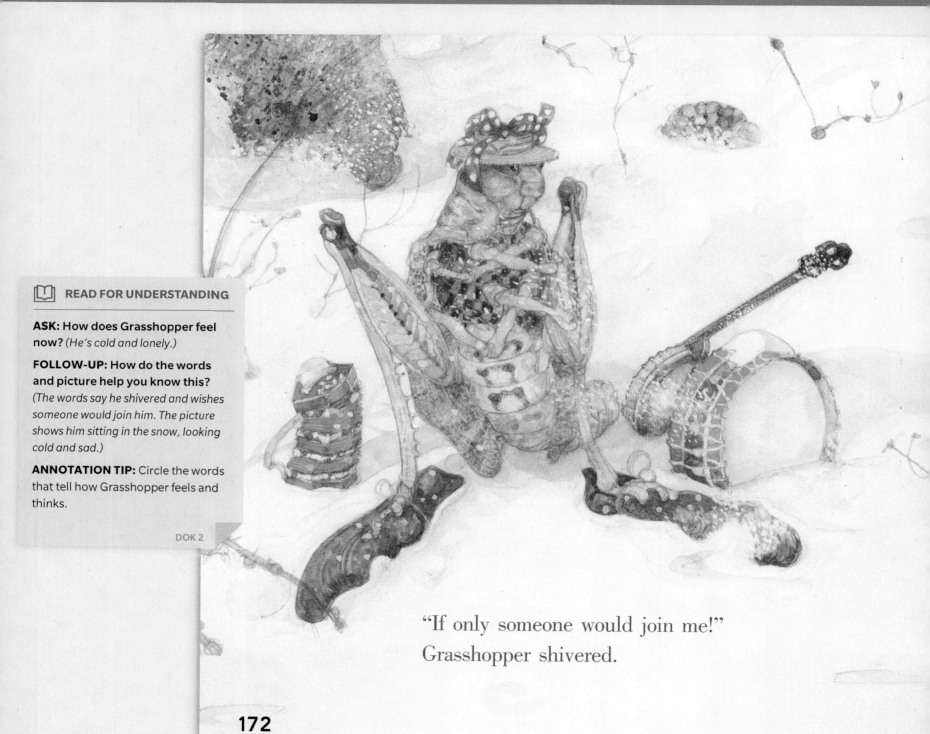

READ FOR UNDERSTANDING

ASK: How does Grasshopper feel now? *(He's cold and lonely.)*

FOLLOW-UP: How do the words and picture help you know this? *(The words say he shivered and wishes someone would join him. The picture shows him sitting in the snow, looking cold and sad.)*

ANNOTATION TIP: Circle the words that tell how Grasshopper feels and thinks.

DOK 2

"If only someone would join me!"
Grasshopper shivered.

172

📖 **READ FOR UNDERSTANDING**

Make Inferences

MODEL MAKING AN INFERENCE

🔍 **THINK ALOUD** *I know that Grasshopper is cold. I see him walking through the snow toward the Ants' house. I also know that it is warm inside people's houses in the winter because they heat them. I can use these clues to make an inference. I think Grasshopper is going to ask the Ants if he can go inside with them.*

DOK 2

173

175

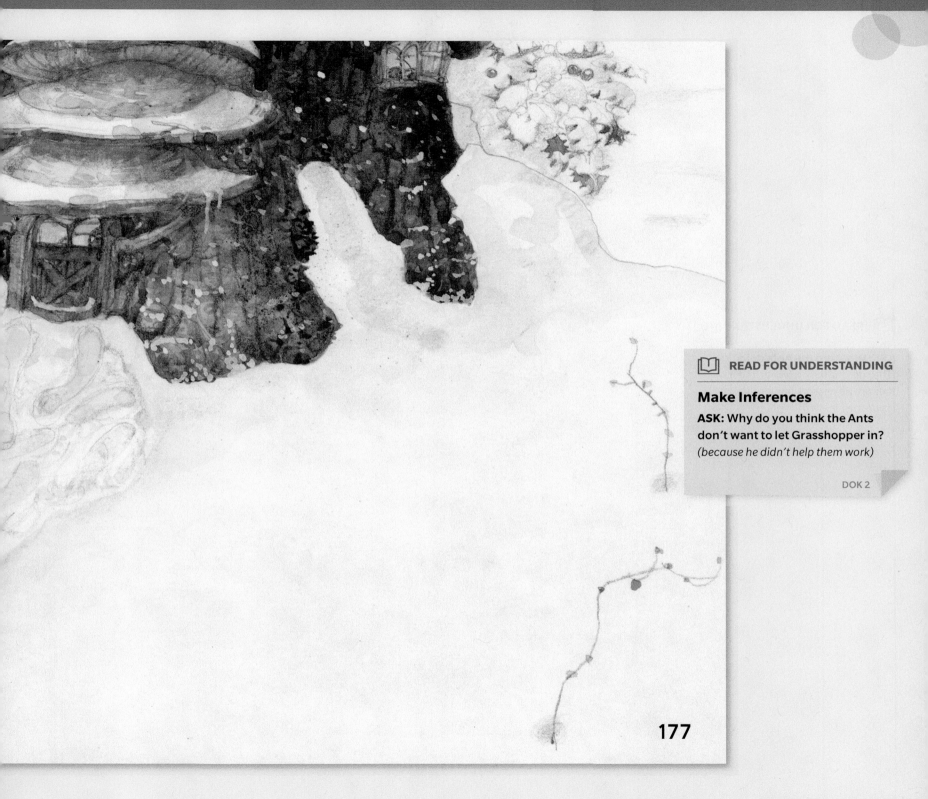

📖 READ FOR UNDERSTANDING

Make Inferences

ASK: Why do you think the Ants don't want to let Grasshopper in?
(because he didn't help them work)

DOK 2

177

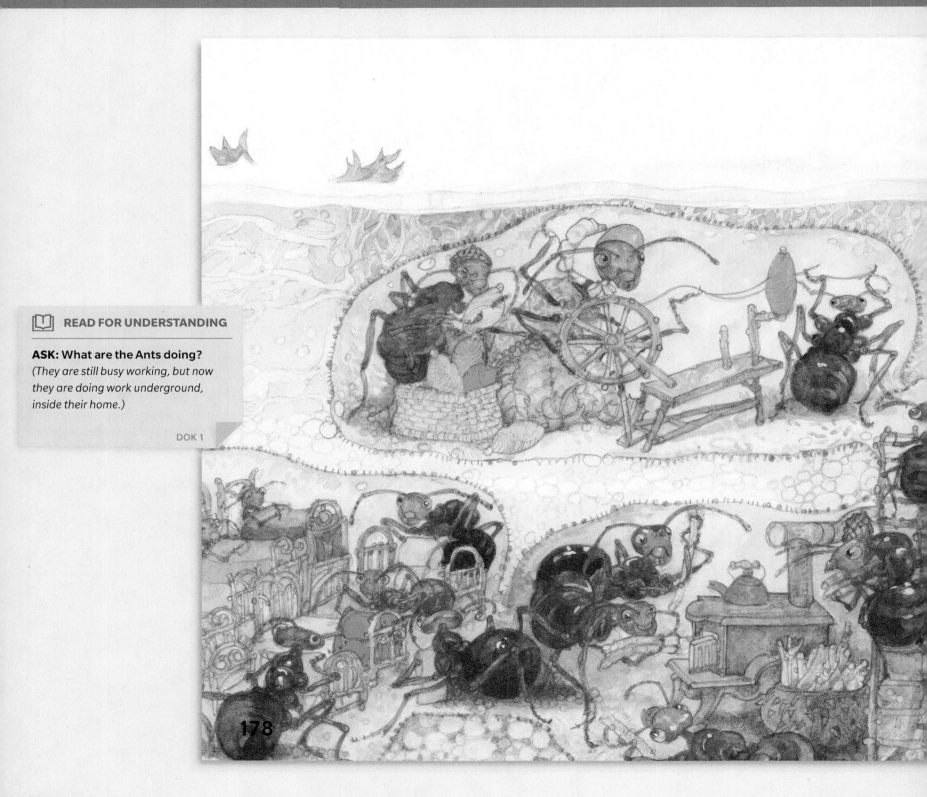

📖 **READ FOR UNDERSTANDING**

ASK: What are the Ants doing?
(They are still busy working, but now they are doing work underground, inside their home.)

DOK 1

178

READ FOR UNDERSTANDING

ASK: What is Grasshopper doing? *(He is still sitting alone outside in the snow.)*

FOLLOW-UP: What do you think Grasshopper learned from the Ants? *(that it's important to do your share of the work)*

DOK 2

179

180

"A cup of tea?" asked Queen Ant.
"How kind of you," said Grasshopper.

181

182

183

Wrap Up

Revisit the predictions children made before reading. Have them confirm or correct their predictions using evidence from the text and pictures.

DOK 2

184

READ Together

Turn and Talk

Use details from **The Grasshopper & the Ants** to answer these questions with a partner.

1. **Make Inferences** What do the grasshopper and the ants learn from each other?

2. Do you think the ants should share with the grasshopper? Why or why not?

Talking Tip

Complete the sentence to add to what your partner says.

My idea is _____.

185

Write a Description

PROMPT How does Grasshopper change during the story? Use details from the words and pictures to explain your ideas.

PLAN Describe what Grasshopper is like at the beginning, middle, and end of the story.

Beginning	Middle	End

Write About Reading

- **Read aloud** the prompt.
- **Lead a discussion** in which children share their ideas about how Grasshopper changes from the beginning of the story to the end. Tell them to use text evidence to support their ideas.
- Then read aloud the Plan section. Have children use ideas from the discussion as they write.

DOK 3

WRITE Now write sentences to describe how Grasshopper changes. Remember to:

- Tell about Grasshopper's actions and feelings at the beginning, middle, and end of the story.

- Use describing words.

Responses may vary.

187

Independent Close Reading

Have children close read and annotate "A Tale of Two Mice" on their own during small-group or independent work time. As needed, **use the Scaffolded Support notes** that follow to guide children who need additional help.

Scaffolded Support

As needed, remind children to:

- use clues from the words and pictures, as well as what they already know, to make a smart guess about what lesson the mice will learn.

- think about their predictions and see if they are correct. DOK 2

Prepare to Read

GENRE STUDY **Fables** have been told for many years and teach a lesson.

MAKE A PREDICTION Preview **A Tale of Two Mice**. You know fables teach a lesson. What lesson do you think the mice will learn in this fable?

They will learn that it is better to live in the same place.

SET A PURPOSE Read to find out what happens when the mice visit each other and to see if your prediction is right.

A Tale of Two Mice

READ What is the city like? <u>Underline</u> words that describe it.

Country Mouse got an e-mail from his friend. "Come visit me in the city!" it said.

So Country Mouse took a bike, a bus, and a train. At last, he got to the big city. It was so busy! People rushed past. Loud horns honked. Country Mouse was scared! ▶

Close Reading Tip

Is your prediction right so far? If not, think about what fables are like and make a new prediction.

CHECK MY UNDERSTANDING

Describe the city and how Country Mouse feels about it.

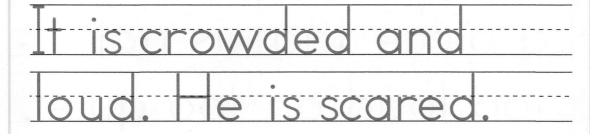

It is crowded and loud. He is scared.

189

Scaffolded Support

As needed, guide children to:

- think about and describe what the city is like.
- use details in the words and picture to figure out how Country Mouse feels about the city.
- confirm and revise predictions as they read.

DOK 2

Close Reading Tip

Put a ! by a surprising part.

Scaffolded Support

As needed, remind children to:

• think about how the setting has changed, which words tell about it, and why it is important to the story.

• use clues in the text and pictures to make a smart guess about something the author does not say.

DOK 2

READ <u>Underline</u> words that describe the new setting.

Country Mouse texted City Mouse. "I'm going home! Please come visit *me!*"

So City Mouse took a train, a bus, and a bike. When he got to the country, he saw no one. It was silent. He felt nervous.

City Mouse texted his friend. "This place is too quiet for me! Why don't we meet someplace in the middle?"

CHECK MY UNDERSTANDING

Why does City Mouse want to meet Country Mouse someplace in the middle?

They might both like a place that is not too loud or too quiet.

190

WRITE ABOUT IT What lesson do you think the mice learn? Write sentences to tell about it.

Cite Text Evidence

It's okay for friends to like different things.

Scaffolded Support

As needed, guide children to use clues in the text and pictures to help them figure out the lesson the mice learn.

DOK 3

191

 READ FOR UNDERSTANDING

Introduce the Text

- **Read aloud** and discuss the information about the genre.
- **Guide children** to set a purpose for reading to practice synthesizing important ideas.
- **Provide information** about the author, Helen Lester.
- **Tell children** to look for and think about the Power Words as they read.

Prepare to Read

GENRE STUDY **Informational text** is nonfiction. It gives facts about a topic. Look for:

- facts about people
- photographs of real people

SET A PURPOSE Read to find out the most important ideas in each part. Then **synthesize**, or put the ideas together in your mind, to find out new things about the text and what it really means to you.

POWER WORDS
nonsense
wise
lesson
tale
reply

Meet Helen Lester.

192

Thank You, Mr. Aesop

by Helen Lester

illustrated by
Roberto Weigand

📖 **READ FOR UNDERSTANDING**

Make Predictions

- **Page through** the beginning of *Thank You, Mr. Aesop* with children.
- Have them **use prior knowledge,** the illustrations, and photos to predict what the selection will be about. Tell children they will **return to their predictions** after they finish reading the selection.

DOK 2

📖 **READ FOR UNDERSTANDING**

Concept Words

As children read *Thank You, Mr. Aesop,* they may see familiar words from their speaking and listening vocabularies that they may not know how to read yet. Write these words on the board, read them aloud, and discuss their meanings as needed.

- Aesop
- author
- fables
- retell
- stories

Synthesize

MODEL SYNTHESIZING

💬 **THINK ALOUD** *When I synthesize, I think about the important things I read in a text and what it all means to me. The important things I read here are that long ago, a man named Aesop told stories that taught people lessons. I wonder if I have ever heard or read one of his stories. I'll remember this idea as I keep reading.*

DOK 3

🔍 **TARGETED CLOSE READ**

Central Idea

Have children reread pages 194–195 to analyze the text's central idea.

ASK: Who is this text mostly about? *(Aesop)*

FOLLOW-UP: What does the author tell you about Aesop? *(He was a storyteller who lived long, long ago.)*

DOK 2

Aesop lived a long, long time ago. It was SO LONG AGO that we are not even sure he was real! Some people think Aesop was a storyteller from Greece who told stories about animals that acted like people. Some animals were full of nonsense. Others were wise.

These stories are called *fables*. Each one teaches a lesson.

194

People liked Aesop's fables. One person told the story to another . . . who told another . . . who told another. . . . You get the idea!

Long after Aesop's time, people were still telling the fables. They were printed in books. Each author changed the story to make it a little different.

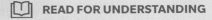
195

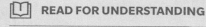

READ FOR UNDERSTANDING

Phonics/Decoding in Context

Have children point to the word *art*. Review how the letters *ar* stand for the /är/ sound. Model blending the sounds in the word: /är/ /t/, *art*. Have children repeat.

READ FOR UNDERSTANDING

Synthesize

MODEL SYNTHESIZING

◯ **THINK ALOUD** *Authors are still telling Aesop's fables. Jerry Pinkney is one of them. I know that he uses his art to tell the story. Since people still read Aesop's stories, I can synthesize that authors write new versions so we can continue to enjoy the stories and learn from them.*

DOK 3

Today, people still like Aesop's fables! Many authors retell these stories. The author Jerry Pinkney wrote his own versions of Aesop's fables. His art helps to tell each tale.

196

Notice **&** Note

Contrasts and Contradictions

- **Remind children** that when they are reading and two things contrast, they should stop to notice and note.

- **Have children explain** why they might use this strategy on pages 196–197. (*Authors tell Aesop's fables in different ways. This means that the same story can be told with new details.*)

ANNOTATION TIP: Have children circle the things that contrast on these pages.

- **Remind children** of the Anchor Question: **What does this make me wonder about?** (*Possible response: I wonder why the authors would have the characters act in different ways.*)

DOK 2

Ed Emberley and his daughter Rebecca also retell Aesop's fables. They change the stories to make them their own. In their book <u>The Ant and the Grasshopper</u>, the weather is hot, not cold like in other versions. Also, the grasshopper is not alone. He plays music with a bug band!

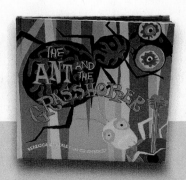

📖 **READ FOR UNDERSTANDING**

Quick Teach Words

As needed to support comprehension, briefly explain the meaning of *versions* and *alone* in this context.

- If there are two *versions* of a story, there are two different ways the story is told.

- If you are *alone*, you are not with anyone else.

197

Central Idea

Have children reread page 198 to analyze the text's central idea.

ASK: What does the author want you to learn from this text? (*Some stories have been told over and over for many years.*)

FOLLOW-UP: What evidence lets you know? (*The text says that Aesop was a storyteller that lived long ago and that his stories are still being told by different authors today.*)

DOK 3

📖 **READ FOR UNDERSTANDING**

Wrap Up

Revisit the predictions children made before reading. Have them confirm or correct their predictions using evidence from the text and pictures.

DOK 2

Think of it! Many fables we know were first told long, LONG ago. These stories hold lessons for us all.

So, will YOU be the next storyteller? I hope your reply is "Yes!" You could retell an old fable or make up a new one. What lesson will it teach?

198

Turn and Talk

Use details from **Thank You, Mr. Aesop** to answer these questions with a partner.

1. **Synthesize** Why do you think Aesop's fables have been told over and over for so long?

2. How are Jerry Pinkney's stories different from Aesop's?

Talking Tip

Ask a question if you are not sure about your partner's ideas.

Why did you say _____?

Academic Discussion

Use the TURN AND TALK routine.
Remind children to listen carefully to their partner and to ask questions to clarify anything they do not understand.

Possible responses:

1. *People like his stories. The lessons in the stories are still important for people to learn today.* DOK 3

2. *Jerry Pinkney uses art to tell the stories. Aesop told his stories out loud.* DOK 2

199

Write Facts

PROMPT What are the most interesting facts you learned from **Thank You, Mr. Aesop**? Look back at the sentences and pictures for ideas.

PLAN First, write notes about the facts, or true information, you learned about Aesop, fables, and authors.

WRITE Now write three of the most interesting facts you learned from **Thank You, Mr. Aesop**. Remember to:

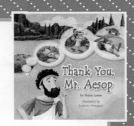

- Tell true information.

- Make sure each sentence tells a complete idea and ends with an end mark.

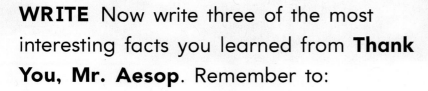

Responses may vary.

201

Prepare to Read

GENRE STUDY **Informational text** is nonfiction. It gives facts about a topic.

MAKE A PREDICTION Preview **Make Stories Come Alive**. You know that an informational text has facts. What do you think you will learn?

I will learn facts about how to tell an exciting story.

SET A PURPOSE Read to find out how to tell a story for others to enjoy.

202

Make Stories Come Alive

READ What do storytellers do? <u>Underline</u> the words that tell.

Do you know a good storyteller? Good storytellers make you want to listen. They can make you laugh. They tell stories that make you feel excited, sad, or scared.

Telling a story isn't hard! You can do it, too. It just takes time and some practice. ▶

Close Reading Tip

Mark important ideas with *.

Scaffolded Support

As needed, remind children to:

- look for facts, or things the author says that can be proven or checked.

- think about which ideas are most important and why.

DOK 2

CHECK MY UNDERSTANDING

What is the most important thing you learn on this page?

It takes practice to be a good storyteller.

203

Close Reading Tip

Circle words you don't know. Then figure them out.

Scaffolded Support

As needed, remind children that:

- details are the facts or ideas that the author gives about a topic.

- they should use details in the text to figure out the central idea.

DOK 3

READ Which details tell how to be a good storyteller? Underline them.

Here are some storytelling tips. First, pick a story you like. Then tell it out loud. Speak clearly. Use different voices for the characters. You can also use your body to act out the story. Practice telling it a few times.

Then share your story. You could tell it to a group or make a video for people to watch. Make it funny or exciting! Remember to have fun. Make your story come alive!

CHECK MY UNDERSTANDING

What is the main idea, or central idea, of the whole text?

It's about how to tell a story well so that others will enjoy it.

204

WRITE ABOUT IT Write the title of a story you would like to tell. Then write things you learned that you will do to make your story lively and exciting when you tell it.

Responses will vary but should include some ideas from the text.

205

Prepare to View

GENRE STUDY **Videos** are short movies. Some videos give information. Others are for you to watch for enjoyment. Watch and listen for:

• the lesson the video teaches

• how the pictures, words, and sounds work together to tell a story

SET A PURPOSE Watch to find out who the **characters** are and what they look like. Find out what the characters do, say, and feel to help you understand why they act as they do.

Build Background: Tortoises and Hares

206

The Tortoise and the Hare

VIEW FOR UNDERSTANDING

Make Predictions

- **Display** the cover of *The Tortoise and the Hare* for children.

- Have children **use prior knowledge** and the opening page to predict what the video will be about. Tell children they will **return to their predictions** after they finish watching the video.

DOK 2

from Speakaboos, adapted by Amy Kraft

As You View Use the pictures and words to find out what the tortoise and hare are like. What do they do? Look for details to help you understand why the characters act the way they do. What lessons do they learn?

 VIEW FOR UNDERSTANDING

Characters

ASK: What are the tortoise and the hare like? *(The hare is arrogant and fast; the tortoise is wise and slow.)*

FOLLOW-UP: Why does each one run the race the way they do? *(The hare thinks she will win, so she doesn't put a lot of effort into the race; the tortoise is patient and runs a steady race.)*

DOK 2

A whistle blew, and they were off. The hare sprinted down the road while the tortoise crawled away from the starting line.

208

Use details from **The Tortoise and the Hare** to answer these questions with a partner.

1. **Characters** Describe the hare. Why does the hare stop to rest during the race?

2. What lesson does the hare learn after the race?

Talking Tip

Speak loudly enough so that your partner can hear you. Do not speak too fast or too slow.

I think that _____.

209

READ
Together

Let's Wrap Up!

(?) Essential Question

What lessons can we learn from stories?

Pick one of these activities to show what you have learned about the topic.

1. Make a Badge

Make a badge. Draw a picture on it that shows a lesson you learned from the stories. Write a sentence to tell how to earn the badge.

Revisit the Essential Question

- **Read aloud** the Essential Question.
- **Remind children** that in this module, they read different texts about lessons stories can teach us that can help them answer the question.
- **Have children** choose one of the activities to show what they learned in this module.

Make a Badge

- **Guide children** to revisit the stories they read and think about the lessons they learned.
- **Encourage children** to share their badges in a small group and explain how their badges can be earned.

DOK 3

2. Guessing Game

Choose a character from the stories. Think about the lesson the character learned. Act out something the character would do. Have a partner guess the character.

Word Challenge

Can you use the word amuse to tell about the character?

Play a Guessing Game

- **Guide children** to describe their actions as they act out the lesson. For example, they can say *I'll try again* or *I'm getting ready for winter.*
- **Encourage them** to use the Big Idea Word *amuse* when they describe their actions.

DOK 3

Brainstorm and Plan

Have children use the My Notes space to jot down ideas for their chosen activity. Remind them to refer back to their notes as they complete the activity.

My Notes

211

Glossary

A

affect   If things **affect** something else, they change it in some way.
How does the hot sun **affect** how you feel?

amuse   If you **amuse** people, you make them smile or laugh.
We did a funny play to **amuse** our parents.

autumn   **Autumn** is the season after summer and before winter.
In **autumn**, leaves change color and fall from the trees.

amuse

autumn

B

boldly   If you do something **boldly**, you do it in a way that is confident or not polite.
She **boldly** took the toy when it was not her turn to use it.

break   A **break** is a short rest.
We took a **break** after working hard at soccer practice.

break

C

chirped   If someone **chirped**, they said something in a happy, lively way.
The girl **chirped** about the great show she just saw.

chirped

213

cycle A **cycle** is a group of events that repeat in the same order.
The seasons come one after another in a **cycle**.

D

direction

direction A **direction** is the certain way or path that someone goes along.
When we went hiking, we walked in the **direction** of the lake.

dunes

dunes Dunes are hills of sand in a desert or by the ocean.
We walked up and down the sand **dunes** at the beach.

E

edges   The **edges** of something are the places where it ends.
The two teams stood along the **edges** of the field.

entertain   When you want to **entertain** people, you could act, sing, or dance.
The children **entertain** us by dancing in the parade.

entertain

evaporation   **Evaporation** is when something gets very hot and turns into a gas.
In the hot pot, **evaporation** made some of the water go away.

evaporation

F

follow   When you **follow** someone, you walk behind that person to go to the same place.
Baby ducks **follow** their mother to the pond.

215

fossils

fossils Fossils are what is left of plants and animals from long ago and can be found in rocks.

Some **fossils** are dinosaur bones or look like shells or leaves.

H

hike When you **hike**, you go on a long walk.

It takes a long time to **hike** to the lake.

I

interrupt When you **interrupt** someone, you stop that person from talking.

If you **interrupt** me, I won't be able to tell you the rest of the story.

hike

involved If you are **involved** in something, you join in and feel strongly about it.
He got **involved** in telling a story to us and made it exciting.

L

labor When you **labor**, you work.
When we **labor** in the garden, we pull weeds and water the plants.

landed If something **landed**, it came down to the ground.
The jet **landed** at the airport.

lesson A **lesson** is something important you learn.
We learned a **lesson** about why it is good to share.

labor

landed

217

liquid

literature

liquid   A **liquid** is something that you can pour, like water or milk.

I pour the **liquid** to fill up each part.

literature   Stories, plays, and poems are all kinds of **literature**.

My teacher gives us good **literature** to read.

M

mission   A **mission** is an important job you do.

Our **mission** is to paint the fence.

N

nonsense   If something is **nonsense**, it is silly or not true.

The silly fox in the story was full of **nonsense**.

218

P

popular   If something is **popular**, many people know about it and like it.
All of us want to play the **popular** game.

problem   A **problem** is something that is hard to figure out.
The dog's **problem** is that it cannot reach the ball.

problem

R

relaxing   When you are **relaxing**, you are resting.
After work, he is **relaxing** at his house.

reply   A **reply** is an answer to a question.
My **reply** to your question is "Yes!"

relaxing

219

rest   When you **rest**, you are quiet, don't do anything, and might sleep.
We **rest** after playing all day.

rim   A **rim** is the place where something ends, or the edge of it.
We walk along the **rim** and see a river down below.

rim

S

shrubs   **Shrubs** are bushes, which are woody plants with lots of stems and are smaller than trees.
We planted small **shrubs** by our house.

sly   A person who is **sly** is smart and might have a secret.
In the story, the tricky fox had a **sly** look on its face.

shrubs

220

spectacular   If something is **spectacular**, it is very big and exciting to look at.
That **spectacular** waterfall is so big!

spines   If something has **spines**, it has thin, pointed parts that are sharp.
Don't touch the sharp **spines** on the cactus plant!

storyteller   A **storyteller** is a person who writes or tells a story.
The **storyteller** told a funny story to our class.

supposed   If you are **supposed** to do something, you should do it.
We are **supposed** to do our homework.

spectacular

storyteller

221

T

tale

tale   A **tale** is a story.
We read a **tale** about a little red hen.

trace   To **trace** something, you draw a line around the outside of it.
Trace around your hand to make a picture of your hand.

W

trace

warn   When you **warn** people, you let them know about danger.
The police officer will **warn** drivers if the roads get icy.

wise   If you are **wise**, you use what you know to make good decisions.
The **wise** leader helped us pick the best place to camp.

Index of Titles and Authors

Arnold, Quinn M. 36

Barnett, Mac 14

Bazillions, The 92

"Be a Bird Helper" 69

Deserts 36

Ernst, Lisa Campbell 138

Follow the Story Path 102

Gilbert, Sara 72

Grand Canyon 72

"Grand Canyon Fossils" 89

Grasshopper & the Ants, The 162

Handmade 58

"Hansel and Gretel Two" 135

"How an Island Is Made" 55

Interrupting Chicken 104

"Keep Trying" 159

Kraft, Amy 206

Lester, Helen 192

Little Red Riding Hood 138

"Make Stories Come Alive" 203

Pinkney, Jerry 162

Rodríguez, Guadalupe 58

"Ron and Tron" 33

Sam & Dave Dig a Hole 14

Stein, David Ezra 104

Storm Report 12

"Tale of Two Mice, A" 189

Thank You, Mr. Aesop 192

Tortoise and the Hare, The 206

Water Cycle 92

Acknowledgments

Cover illustration from *The Ant and the Grasshopper* by Rebecca Emberley and Ed Emberley. Copyright © 2012 by Rebecca Emberley Inc. Reprinted by permission of Macmillan Publishing Company.

Cover illustration from *The Crocodile and the Scorpion* by Rebecca Emberley and Ed Emberley. Copyright © 2013 by Rebecca Emberley and Ed Emberley. Reprinted by permission of Roaring Brook Press, a division of Holtzbrinck Publishing Holdings Limited Partnership.

Cover illustration from *The Lion & the Mouse* by Jerry Pinkney. Copyright © 2009 by Jerry Pinkney. Reprinted by permission of Little, Brown Books for Young Readers, a division of Hachette Book Group, Inc.

Cover illustration from *The Tortoise & the Hare* by Jerry Pinkney. Copyright © 2013 by Jerry Pinkney. Reprinted by permission of Little, Brown Books for Young Readers, a division of Hachette Book Group, Inc.

Deserts by Quinn M. Arnold. Text copyright © 2017 by Creative Education and Creative Paperbacks. Creative Education and Creative Paperbacks are imprints of The Creative Company, Mankato, MN 56001 USA. Reprinted by permission of The Creative Company.

Grand Canyon by Sara Gilbert. Text copyright © 2017 by Sara Gilbert. Reprinted by permission of Creative Education, an imprint of The Creative Company, Mankato, MN 56001 USA.

The Grasshopper & the Ants by Jerry Pinkney. Copyright © 2015 by Jerry Pinkney. Reprinted by permission of Hachette Book Group USA and Sheldon Fogelman.

"Landscape with an Animal" (retitled from "Paisaje con animal"),"Flying Fish" (retitled from "Pez volador"), and "Paper Birds" (retitled from "Pájaros en papel") from *Handmade* (retitled from *Hecho a Mano*) by Guadalupe Rodríguez. Copyright © 2009 by Guadalupe Rodríguez. Reprinted by permission of Editorial Amanuta Limitada and b small publishing.

Interrupting Chicken by David Ezra Stein. Copyright © 2010 by David Ezra Stein. Reprinted by permission of Candlewick Press, Somerville, MA, Editorial Juventud, and Recorded Books.

Sam & Dave Dig a Hole by Mac Barnett, illustrated by Jon Klassen. Text copyright © 2014 by Mac Barnett. Illustration copyright © 2014 by Jon Klassen. Reprinted by permission of Candlewick Press, Somerville, MA.

Credits

4 (top girl) ©Houghton Mifflin Harcourt, (top bg) ©lukeruk/Shutterstock, (b) ©Hoang Bao Nguyen/Dreamstime; 5 (c) ©Frank Krahmer/Corbis Documentary/Getty Images, (b) ©2015 by The Bazillions; 7 (b) ©Homer Learning; 8 ©Andrew Mayovskyy/Shutterstock, 12 (bg) ©Vladimir Gjorgiev/Shutterstock, (fg) ©Astarina/Shutterstock; 13 (b) ©Photo Researchers/Science Source/Getty Images, (tr) ©Pavliha/E+/Getty Images, (cr) ©J. Pat Carter/AP Images, (tl) ©Maciej Nicgorski/EyeEm/Getty Images, (cl) ©Fred Zhang/Moment/Getty Images; 14 ©Moranne Keeler/Candlewick Press, Inc.; 36 ©imageBROKER/Alamy; 37 ©Hoang Bao Nguyen/Dreamstime; 38 ©Eastmanphoto/Dreamstime; 39 ©Valentin Armianu/Dreamstime; 40 ©Zeusthegr8/Dreamstime; 41 ©Ann & Steve Toon/Robert Harding/Getty Images; 42 ©Dragonika/Dreamstime; 43 (inset) ©Lirtlon/Dreamstime, (bg) ©Gallo Images/Danita Delimont/Getty Images; 44 ©moodboard/Alamy; 45 ©Cultura/Philip Lee Harvey/Getty Images; 46 ©PaulVinten/iStockPhoto.com; 47 (t) ©ebettini/iStockPhoto.com, (b) ©Havranka/Dreamstime; 48 (bg) ©Alex7370/Dreamstime, (inset) ©Pleprakaymas/Dreamstime; 49 (bg) ©Tom Roche/Shutterstock, (tr) ©fivespots/Shutterstock, (tl) ©Stuart Dee/Photographer's Choice RF/Getty Images; 50 ©Martin Maun/Dreamstime; 54 ©Christian Wilkinson/Alamy; 56 ©Christian Wilkinson/Alamy; 58 ©SolStock/E+/Getty Images; 72 (b) ©Benny Marty/Shutterstock, (bg) ©Frank Krahmer/Corbis Documentary/Getty Images; 73 (bg) ©Frank Krahmer/Corbis Documentary/Getty Images, (inset) ©Wisconsinart/Dreamstime; 74 (bg) ©Christian Beier/CBpictures/Alamy, (inset) ©Wisconsinart/Dreamstime; 76 ©Inge Johnsson/Alamy; 77 (bg) ©George H.H. Huey/Alamy, (inset) ©Wisconsinart/Dreamstime; 78 (tr) ©Michael Quinn/National Park Service/Grand Canyon National Park, (b) ©Derek Von Briesen/National Geographic Magazines/Getty Images; 79 (bg) ©Mark Miller/Alamy, (inset) ©Wisconsinart/Dreamstime; 80 (tr) ©Joel W. Rogers/Corbis Documentary/Getty Images, (b) ©Scott Smith/Corbis Documentary/Getty Images; 81 (bg) ©Pacific Northwest Photo/Shutterstock, (inset) ©Wisconsinart/Dreamstime; 82 (inset) ©taviphoto/Shutterstock, (bg) ©Ronnie Howard/Shutterstock; 83 ©Neale Clark/Robert Harding/Getty Images; 84 (t) ©Danny Smythe/Shutterstock, (b) ©Anna Kucherova/Shutterstock, (inset) ©Wisconsinart/Dreamstime; 88 ©Michele Falzone/AWL Images/Getty Images; 89 (l), (r) ©Michael Quinn/National Park Service/Grand Canyon National Park, (inset) ©mgkaya/iStockPhoto.com;